The Contemporary American Family

The Contemporary American Family

A Dialectical Perspective on Communication and Relationships

Teresa Chandler Sabourin

University of Cincinnati

SAGE Publications
International Educational and Professional Publisher
Thousand Oaks ■ London ■ New Delhi

For information:

Sage Publications, Inc.
2455 Teller Road
Thousand Oaks, California 91320
E-mail: order@sagepub.com

Sage Publications Ltd.
6 Bonhill Street
London EC2A 4PU
United Kingdom

Sage Publications India Pvt. Ltd.
B-42 Panchsheel Enclave
New Delhi 110 017 India

Printed in the United States of America

Library of Congress Cataloging-in-Publication Data

Sabourin, Teresa Chandler.
The contemporary American family: a dialectical perspective / by Teresa Chandler Sabourin.
    p. cm.
Includes bibliographical references and index.
ISBN 0-7619-2445-0 — ISBN 0-7619-2446-9 (pbk.)
    1. Family-United States. 2. Change (Psychology) I. Title.
HQ536 .S213 2003
306.85´0973—dc211

2002152035

03 04 05 10 9 8 7 6 5 4 3 2 1

Acquiring Editor:	Margaret H. Seawell
Production Editor:	Claudia A. Hoffman
Typesetter:	C&M Digitals (P) Ltd.
Indexer:	Molly Hall
Cover Designer:	Janet Foulger

Contents

Acknowledgments

The completion of this book came about through the support and encouragement of many people. First, I would like to thank my colleagues in the Department of Communication at the University of Cincinnati: Gail Fairhurst, Steve Depoe, Barbara Reckers, and Nuha Nasrallah. I am also indebted to the graduate and undergraduate students who have shared their wisdom and diversity with me.

Special thanks go to my Sage editor, Margaret Seawell, for her continuing interest and confidence in this project. I would also like to thank Claudia Hoffman, my production editor, and Cheryl Adam, my copy editor, for their help in getting the manuscript into top form.

I wish also to thank my family of origin, the Chandlers. My parents, Mary Lou and Harry, who both passed away in the time since I began this project, always valued and supported my academic goals. My sister and best friend, Julia, has been unwaveringly loyal through both good times and bad. My brother Steve has given me consistent encouragement to follow in our dad's footsteps through my writing. I am also grateful to my sister Susan, whose graciousness has always provided a refuge from life's harsher realities. From afar, my brother Mike has continued to be a source of warmth and light.

Finally, I am grateful beyond belief for being able to share my life with Gary and Clay Sabourin. Throughout this project, they have been constant sources of inspiration, perspective, and good humor.

Preface

❖ HOW I CAME TO WRITE THIS BOOK

For many of us, the inspiration for studying interpersonal communication originated in the history of our own personal relationships. We were drawn to interpersonal studies because we wanted to understand, explain, or improve our friendships, marriage, families, and other long-term relationships. At one time or another, most of us have paused to consider how (or why) some people are drawn together, some stay together, and some pull apart.

— Bochner, Cissna, and Garko, 1990, p. 16

Four experiences encouraged me to question the traditional portrayal of families.

The first happened about 10 year ago when an older student challenged my choice of a text and my emphasis on white, middle-class, nuclear families. At the time, I wasn't the least bit aware of my bias. I considered myself to be an innovator, unafraid to challenge societal norms. Instead, I came to realize that I was a purveyor of the myth of homogeneity. Uncomfortable with and unsure of how to adjust my teaching, I was nonetheless sure I needed to find a way to answer this student's challenge.

My perspective on family life broadened further when I entered a spiritually based recovery program. Here, I found a part of the piece that was missing. I discovered that families affected by chemical dependencies (alcohol, drugs, eating disorders, and others) did not develop or communicate in the same logical ways that were described in the mainstream literature. In my weekly recovery group meetings, I identified more personally with the stories of family life than I ever did during my years of formal study. In the academic literature, a family was one of two things: functional or dysfunctional. There was no in-between. In my own life and the lives of the students that I was teaching, there seemed to be a lot of in between. These gray areas spurred me on to find a way to combine in a meaningful way what I was learning in recovery with my academic knowledge of family life.

The next step on my path was coming across the dialectical way of thinking about family life. During my doctoral program and during subsequent teaching and research as a professor, I found myself specializing in the study of abusive families. From the rational approaches that I had studied formally, abusive families really did not make sense. How can family members both abuse others in their families and care about them at the same time? The literature on men who batter their wives and my forays into the public to discuss abuse as an expert almost always led to the same question: "Why does she stay?" The answers from dualistic approaches did not satisfy.

Then I came across Rawlins's (1992) book on a dialectical approach to friendship. As soon as I read about this perspective as a way to embrace—rather than solve—relational contradictions, I knew I had found my missing piece. I began to read everything I could find on dialectical approaches to friendship. I have since broadened my understanding through reading the works of others who have adopted this way of seeing, and I have applied a dialectical view to my own research and teaching. Even my students, who tend to shrink in the face of theory, can tell that this way of thinking, which validates all manifestations of family structure and culture, has intrinsic merit.

The fourth change that I happened into that again altered my sense of certainty about the ways in which families should be, was to remarry at the age of 35. The man that I married had his own unique background and family experience that did not conform to my prior convictions about how families are. The diversity factor was kicked into even higher gear when our son was born 13 years ago. Parents know how having children makes academic literature seem incomplete as a guide to effective parenting.

As communication experts have evolved in their methods of studying intimate relationships, they have moved from using primarily linear self-reported descriptions of relationships to using more dualistic, observer-based views of dyadic interactions. Although the latter is an improvement on the former, we need to go even further to satisfy our "curiosity about the perplexing dilemmas of social life" (Bochner, Cissna, & Garko, 1990, p. 16). The dialectic perspective, I believe, provides a way to view these dilemmas and gives a direction to proceed in our evolution.

This book is about diversity and the dilemmas of living in families with competing demands. The dialectical approach is a map but not the territory, a powerful tool that allows us to answer the increasing calls that diversity will make on us in the 21st century.

❖ AUDIENCES FOR THE BOOK

Perhaps it is fitting that diverse sources motivated me to write this book. As a teacher of family communication for 18 years, I have been blessed with students of all cultural, racial, and socioeconomic backgrounds. Other texts do not adequately address the diversity I find in my students. I wrote this book for them, and for myself as a teacher so that I could consolidate the materials I have found valuable in our journey of learning about families with diverse structures and cultures.

I also wrote this book because I felt called to take a stand on our society's need to embrace and honor the emerging diversities of our families' structures and cultures. As I teach, I cannot help but recognize that the quality of my students' family experiences does not depend on their families' structural or cultural backgrounds. It would be presumptuous at best and ignorant at worst for me to teach them otherwise. I believe that professionals who work with families—counselors, social workers, ministers, therapists, and others—will find this book thought-provoking and relevant to their concerns about diversity.

Another source of motivation has been my participation in a spiritually based recovery program. There I have heard many stories of family life that defy the neat and tidy descriptions found in most textbooks. Though they come from every type of structural and cultural background imaginable, these families' successes in finding creative ways to deal with potentially devastating adversity have extended my formal education invaluably. I also wish to share my own experiences and understandings with them.

I also hope, in writing this book, to stimulate discussion among scholars and encourage further research on issues of family diversity. As we grow into the new millennium, cultural and structural variations in family life are bound to multiply, and we will need to focus our attention on how to best study and explore these changes.

I hope readers will see this book as an invitation for discussion rather than an argument for "the truth." Although I am very passionate about the materials presented here, I know that they will change and improve as others consider them. If you are a student of the family and want to view contemporary family life in America, this book is for you.

❖ STRUCTURE

I organized the book around seven topics, each related to the main subject of family diversity. Chapter 1 outlines the theoretical perspective of dialectics, adopted here for its eloquence and its power to embrace diversity. Chapter 2 introduces criteria that can account for diversity in definitional procedures. Chapters 3 and 4 deal with some specific examples of structural and cultural diversity, highlighting nuclear, single-parent, and blended families and those families whose members vary in religion, race, or sexual orientation. In Chapter 5, we look at developmental diversity, including both predictable and unpredictable models of family change. Chapters 6 and 7 introduce the concept of functional diversity, which is another way to express how families can become more or less dysfunctional through their life experiences. Chapter 6 focuses on the "dark side" of family life and examines how alcoholism, abuse, and divorce affect the American family. In Chapter 7, we view some of the ways that families' spiritual beliefs and practices serve as resources for facing structural and cultural challenges.

Taken together, these chapters provide a cohesive examination of real families: our diversity, our ways of functioning, our structural makeup, and the communicative resources we use to simultaneously hold our families together and to let them move apart.

1

A Dialectical
Approach to Family

The life of a family is dynamic and changing. Culturally and structurally, "America is made up of a multiplicity of family types, including two-parent families, one-parent families, cohabiting families, gay and lesbian families, and extended-family households" (Teachman, Tedrow, & Crowder, 2000, p. 1234). At the individual level, families can be intimate one moment and distant the next. The family must also maintain a degree of stability while simultaneously adapting to change. These opposing tensions, or connected opposites, are the main focus of a dialectical approach to family communication. Throughout this chapter, I provide an explanation of a dialectical view as a way to understand how families can manage these contradictory tensions. This view emphasizes the family as a whole and recognizes that, instead of an either/or approach, families are both close and distant, stable and changing.

A dialectical approach does not try to solve the contradictions, as some approaches to the family attempt to do, but instead considers the tensions to be a family's true nature, and why it is dynamic, and uncontrollable, in any permanent sense. To accept the contradictions, as a dialectical approach does, is to embrace the family in all of its complexity. As such, adoption of a dialectical view can add to the rich history of knowledge that has been provided by scholars using the theoretical orientations of systems, symbolic interactionism, and social exchange.

> *A dialectical approach does not try to solve the contradictions but considers the tensions to be a family's true nature, and why it is dynamic, and uncontrollable, in any permanent sense.*

The study of family life from a dialectical view may result in the production of as much confusion as clarity and as much uncertainty as sureness. The study of the necessary confusion of family life and its contradictions can shed light on the family processes that are not completely explained by more monologic or linear means. The dialectic approach confronts the notions of prediction and control in the family and instead places the scholar in a dialogue with family. Although the scholar forfeits the illusion of certainty, he or she inherits a vision of how the family adapts and thrives in the midst of uncertainty.

The dialectical approach is to some extent the road less traveled in family communication. Just as some years ago the systems approach, which focuses on observable behaviors, replaced a more monadic conception of family life, which stresses individual-level perceptions, a dialectical approach is likely to become more commonplace as scholars grapple with the non-system features of family in the new millennium. That is, the family today is increasingly diverse in its structure and culture. This diversity means that a family can and does express itself, its membership, and its ways of relating in an infinite array of patterns. Furthermore, this evolving diversity constantly unfolds as families respond to ongoing changes in structure and culture. Diversity, then, is not a static term but references a dynamic process.

According to Allen, Blieszner, and Roberto (2000), "The focus on diversity presents methodological and theoretical problems for researchers" as they "struggle with how to account for increasing complexity in families" (p. 913). Furthermore, "Because the family is said to be the established pattern, persons not conforming to it are, by definition, deviant" (Scanzoni & Marsiglio, 1993, p. 106). Although we now replace the term *deviant* with words such as *alternative* when referring to family lifestyles that are not nuclear, it still "necessarily reinforces the conceptual dichotomy between diversity and the family," shoring up the "functionalist belief that the established pattern is 'better' for society than alternatives" (Scanzoni & Marsiglio, 1993, p. 106).

> *The family today is increasingly diverse in its structure and culture.*

Structures, or configurations of family members and roles, vary in terms of the number and type of parents, children, and prior marriages. The nuclear family structure, which consists of two heterosexual partners, married for the first time, and their biological offspring, is no longer the standard from which to compare other family forms. And although "individuals who cannot or will not participate in the favored family form face powerful stigmas and handicaps" (Coontz, 2000, p. 286), some political and religious leaders have reified the nuclear family. The current census makes it overwhelmingly clear that this form is but one of many. Bernardes (1993) finds that "the scale of divergence from the model of 'the family' is so vast that the very idea of the family is, and always has been, redundant" (p. 35). It is not the "real" family; it is one variation on the theme of family life. In part, then, diversity means that "families are now based more on voluntary ties, choices, and needs than on presumed obligation" (Allen, Blieszner, & Roberto, 2000, p. 913).

Culturally, the ways in which families express their ethnicity, race, sexual orientations, and religion also have enormous variations. Furthermore, some scholars see family theory to be both "a production of culture" and "a reflection of culture" (Bernardes, 1993, p. 38). In the latest census of the U.S. population, a third of the respondents considered themselves to be of mixed cultural heritage (U.S. Census Bureau, 2000). Caucasians are no longer a majority of the population in California, and people in all states are becoming more assimilated into each other's cultural worlds. Again, a claim that only one cultural expression is valid and qualifies as a "real" family is patently false. Families express their membership and culture in a variety of ways, all of which they consider to be real.

> *The nuclear family structure, which consists of two heterosexual partners, married for the first time, and their biological offspring, is no longer the standard from which to compare other family forms.*

The dialectical approach I use to study family diversity here includes three major concepts: change, connection, and contradiction. Consider these terms as conceptual tools.

❖ CONCEPTUAL TOOLS

I mean this selection of concepts to open a way to a dialectical appreciation of family life, and I necessarily exclude some terms that may be highlighted by other dialectically oriented scholars. It is not an exhaustive essay on dialectical thinking but, instead, a useful starting place for applying the approach to the study of family life.

Although rich in history, many dialectical discussions begin with the assumption that social life is complex and open-ended (Baxter & Montgomery, 1996). Accordingly, basic concepts of change, contradiction, and connection are centralized. Although I separately define each of these essential concepts, in operation they all heavily influence each other and are difficult to separate.

In addition, individual scholars from this tradition have created some unique emphases. Baxter and Montgomery (1996), for instance, have identified a set of strategies describing how dialectical tensions are managed in relationships. Another important contribution has been made by Rawlins (1992), who differentiates between contextual dialectics and interactional dialectics in his study of friendship. Whereas contextual dialectics refers to the relationship tensions between the personal and the cultural, interactional dialectics refers to the relationship tensions between persons. Each dialectical type, then, is useful for exploring how families diverge in their cultures and communicative practices. Following a discussion of the basic concepts of change, contradiction, and connection, we will consider management strategies and Rawlins's categories of dialectics in more detail.

Basic Concepts: Change, Connection, Contradiction

Change

The nature of family life is that it is constantly changing. The dialectical conception of change emphasizes its transformational rather than its superficial quality. Transformational change is qualitative, meaning that it is not subject to prediction and control. This is in contrast to a more traditional system's notion of change, which views family as homeostatic, or having a tendency toward balance. The goal of family in systems is to come back to a steady state. But transformational change highlights the creation of a new relationship rather than the restoration of a previous state.

> *The nature of family life is that it is constantly changing.*

The dialectical conception of change provides a different window than the systems approach through which to view family life. Through this window, we can see the creative impact of time on relationships. We can see that time and space are necessary contexts in which to understand meaning in relationships. Also referred to as the chronotopical context, each moment in family life is considered as both a constraint and an enabler of interaction (Baxter & Montgomery, 1996). The stability that the family seeks through routine patterns of relating necessarily creates change because of this shifting chronotopical context. In other words, the same relational dialogue in one time and place will take on new meaning in another. This contrasts with the assumption that change is the "brief interlude separating two steady states" (Montgomery, 1992a, p. 5).

The result of change from this view is dialogic rather than dualistic. Dialogic change emphasizes that relationships are emergent and dependent on the chronotopical contexts for meaning. Dualism sees relationships as changing in a unidirectional manner toward either more of something (e.g., closeness) or less, which is considered its opposite (e.g., distance). The idea that a relationship can be both close and distant simultaneously means that communication, rather than linear development, is the instigator of change. Dualism, then, considers the relationship between opposing forces (dialectical tensions) as an either/or phenomenon. Hence, we would see a family as either in the process of change or in a time of stability. Life cycle models of family development, for example, illustrate the family moving through linear, stable states such as courtship, early marriage, child-rearing, launching, and retirement with only brief, transitional periods of change in between.

A dialogic conception sees the both/and character of stability and change. "Dialectical thinking is not directed toward a search for the 'happy mediums' of compromise and balance, but instead focuses on the messier, less logical, and more inconsistent unfolding practices of the moment" (Baxter & Montgomery, 1996, p. 46). These unfolding practices of the moment are managed through various communication strategies, also called praxical improvisations. The term *praxical improvisation* captures the "in the moment" and emergent nature of dialogic change. Later in this chapter, we will consider some specific management strategies for dealing with change.

Connection

In addition to stability and change, family life involves the constant management of the tension between autonomy and connection. The inherent connectedness of autonomous family members presents interactional challenges. In other words, although all family members are individual autonomous beings with their own personalities, needs, and desires, they are also dependent on a connection to others to survive and to express their autonomy. Thus, the self is a construction of two contradictory necessities, or "the need to connect with another (the centripetal force) and the simultaneous need to separate from the other (centrifugal force)" (Baxter & Montgomery, 1996, p. 25). It is this simultaneity, or a mutual occurrence of autonomy and connection, that we often overlook when we portray family life. Furthermore, being either separate or together cannot resolve the tension of this connection. Instead, it contributes to it. To illustrate, whereas a family may provide for alone-time for its members, at the same time they will always exist within a context of connection. There is not "separate from family" without "connection to family" to differentiate the experience. Dialogically, connection and autonomy exist as a both/and relationship.

Prescriptions for togetherness abound in the family literature. A dualistic notion of closeness implies that a family is either

> *Family life involves the constant management of the tension between autonomy and connection.*

close or distant. In the U.S., society values and considers activities and patterns that indicate closeness as healthy, whereas autonomy is suspect and thought to be a cause of the family's demise. There are many, however, who "challenge 'culture-bound' or essentialist assumptions about the 'right' way to organize family relations and who refute catastrophic claims about collapse of 'the family'" (Coontz, 2000, p. 286).

The political notion of *family values*, "which often includes family affection, intimacy, and sentimentality" (Pyke, 2000, p. 241), demands closeness as a morally correct way to be a family. Accordingly, "in addition to prescribing the structures of families, the family ideal contains notions about the appropriate values, norms, and beliefs that guide the way family members relate to each other" (Pyke, 2000, p. 241). But in a dialogic perspective, separateness and togetherness are contextualized chronotopically—in a constant flow of time and space. It is this chronotopical presence that provides for and enables multiple meanings to emerge as to what it is to be separate and what it is to be together. Thus, the sense of self (i.e., autonomy) defined relationally is subject to flux according to the emergent shared understandings of family members. Family members also construct the sense of connection in an emergent flow. Thus, family members are considered to be "dependent on their relationship, not on one another" (Baxter & Montgomery, 1996, p. 90) for their meanings and their experiences.

A paradox emerging from the dialectical process is that families consist of relationships between autonomous beings where "social phenomena are defined by the relations among their characters, not by the characters themselves" (Montgomery, 1992a, p. 3).

Because members are connected, change processes will always reverberate throughout the family. At the same time, because members have relative autonomy, they will resist and accept change in their own unique ways, thus creating their own unique experiences.

Contradiction

The contradictory nature of relationships is evident in the notions of change and connection. To be both stable and changing, or to be both separate and connected, defies dualistic selection.

The necessary connection between family members exists as a force that is both interdependent and negating. For example, chaos and order both exist in the family. Whereas movement toward order (i.e., routine) may reduce chaos (i.e., novelty), movement toward novelty (change) may disrupt routine (stability). In essence, an abundance of either can negate the other, though they remain interdependent.

A dialectical view of family life accepts the inherent contradictions and does not try to explain them away.

> *Chaos and order both exist in the family.*

Furthermore, because every family experiences these tensions, it is critical to understand how family members manage tensions in their daily interactions. One way to explore the management of contradictions is through the concept of praxis, which "focuses attention on the concrete practices by which social actors produce the future out of the past in their everyday lives" (Baxter & Montgomery, 1996, p. 14). This means that people choose specific language and behavior patterns based on past and present experiences in anticipation of future outcomes. The way that a family experiences and reacts to the inherent dialectical forces, its communicative choices, has an improvisational quality. Thus, praxical improvisations are actions that are in some ways constrained and in some ways enabled by the situation at hand. Social actors both react to and create their ongoing interactional patterns.

Baxter and Montgomery (1996) describe a specific set of praxical patterns that can be used for the interpersonal management of contradictions, such as stability and change.

❖ DIALECTICAL MANAGEMENT PATTERNS

The presence of dialectical tensions requires families to continually negotiate their time, space, and meanings with respect to each other. This time and space, or chronotopical context, is part of the meaning-making process. Although it is unlikely that family members talk explicitly about managing their dialectical tensions, their interactions do result in such management. Baxter and Montgomery (1996) refer to these emergent management patterns as *praxical improvisations* (p. 60). The term *praxical* indicates that action is being taken. The improvisational quality of the actions means that situational givens are used by family members in conjunction with their current communicative choices to create "new" realities. Simply put, to live with the contradictions of family life necessitates ongoing, creative, communicative management. Some of the management patterns appear to be common, although we refer to them by various terms, including selection, separation, neutralization, and reformulation. In the next section, we examine in more detail each of these patterns and their interfaces with culture.

Selection

In order to deal with the presence of dialectical tensions, families sometimes use selection, which is a basic response to contradiction that chooses to emphasize only one polarity. With this pattern, families recognize that the contradiction—both stability and change—exists, but they choose to focus exclusively on one polarity. This approach might be effective under certain conditions, but a continual use of it would indicate denial of the

> *To live with the contradictions of family life necessitates ongoing, creative, communicative management.*

need to attend to both polarities. In essence, the selection pattern indicates that a family responds to their dialectical pressures with a dualistic, either/or approach.

For example, if a family favors novelty to the extreme, eschewing attempts at routine, chaos is likely to ensue. If present on an ongoing basis, chaos, which is an extreme form of change, is generally harmful to family members' development. Conversely, if a family refuses to integrate new information and relies solely on routine as a way to avoid change, it may become rigid, which is not conducive to development either.

Numerous studies show that children, especially, need some degree of structure for everything from bedtime routine to consistent parenting. Likewise, because life presents families with unpredictable events, families must be able to adapt to change. The family that has selected stability as its modus operandi will be more greatly challenged by such demands for change than will other families. A family that has settled on stability to the exclusion of change will meet even predictable change, such as the aging of a child from toddlerhood through puberty, with resistance. Because change is a constant, from a dialectical view, a family's consistent failure to accommodate it will result in less than beneficial outcomes. Likewise, without some routine, family members may not grow as readily as they may in a family that chose to allow for both stability and change.

Separation

The pattern of separation recognizes the interdependence of dialectical polarities but attempts to separate them either temporally (in time) or topically (in a given domain). A family practicing temporal separation might say, "We will be autonomous during the week and connected on the weekends." This strategy specifies a time for both autonomy and connection but holds at bay the fact of their simultaneity. Topical separation, on the other hand, designates spatial domains for polar opposites by relegating autonomy, for example, to personal decisions and relegating connection to decisions affecting the whole family.

This response to dialectical contradictions reflects a practical approach in which the family admits and attempts to meet competing needs. Because families can separate dialectical tensions only temporarily, this approach is not a permanent solution to the tension. If a family forgets that, the members may become frustrated at the eventual failure of their attempt to manage via separation. The management of together- and alone-time is one that constantly challenges families and requires negotiation, sometimes via topical separation in which activity domains are used to identify management patterns.

Neutralization

A common notion about healthy family functioning is that the family achieves a balance between stability and change or togetherness and separateness. Family therapists suggest that a balanced family, one that attempts to be moderate in both stability/change and autonomy/connection, provides the most conducive conditions for healthy development (Olson, Sprenkle, & Russell, 1979). However, this notion of balance as a steady state ignores the inherent and persistent nature of the dialectical tension that makes balance precarious at best. As previously discussed, the notion of balance or homeostasis, as used in systems theory, implies that a steady state is both achievable and desirable. The degree of balance can also vary, with some patterns favoring togetherness and others favoring autonomy. The more extreme form of connection is called enmeshment, in which no boundary between self and other is recognized. The more extreme form of autonomy is disengagement. These extremes are examples of selection in which one polarity is, in effect, ignored. This means that neutralization, like the other praxical improvisations, may be effective in a given time and place, but, if relied on exclusively, will transform into the very thing that it intends to avoid: extremity. Constant neutralization, then, can serve to deny change. For practical purposes, however, families do attempt to cope with dialectical forces through neutralization, striving for moderation or a middle ground between the poles. By choosing to neutralize competing needs, a family indicates that it perceives the contrasting poles but attempts to diminish the intensity of their force.

One common way families manage tension through neutralization is compromise, in which members sacrifice a portion of each dialectical element. The nature of the compromise, which may consistently favor one polarity, determines the degree of togetherness or separateness.

> *This notion of balance as a steady state ignores the inherent and persistent nature of the dialectical tension that makes balance precarious at best.*

Reformulation

This strategy is one in which the existing tension of opposites is redefined so as to transform the opposites into a unified whole. Through this process of reframing, families negotiate a new reality that transcends the contrast of oppositional forces. Reformulation requires a perceptual transformation to occur so that, for example, families experience separateness as ultimate connection. In his book *Soulmates*, Moore (1994) proposes that the ultimate intimacy arises from protecting each other's solitude in marriage. Another family may be so extreme in its traditionalism that it appears to be unique from other families.

Although reformulation, also called *recalibration* (Baxter & Montgomery, 1996, p. 65), "transcends the form in which an opposition is expressed," it does not permanently resolve the contradiction. Thus, like other patterns of managing dialectical pressures in family life, reformulation is, at best, temporarily effective and, at worst, an indirect expression of denial.

Each of these four patterns—selection, separation, neutralization, and reformulation—can be temporarily effective in negotiating contradictions. None of them, however, can ultimately resolve the contradictions that are constant and in flux such that a pattern that works in one time and place is rendered meaningless in another. This may cause great confusion among family members who seek permanent solutions to the strains of family life and may often attempt to "be like we used to be"

> *To successfully manage dialectical pressures in family life is to remain open and responsive to the emerging present, which is itself in dialectical tension with the past and the future.*

despite changing circumstances. Older couples who reminisce about their falling-in-love days, for example, may miss the beauty of the current state of their relationships by focusing only on how they used to be, not what they are now. To successfully manage dialectical pressures in family life is to remain open and responsive to the emerging present, which is itself in dialectical tension with the past and the future. Montgomery (1992a) likens it to riding a unicycle, when "adjustments serve to transform the relationship from one moment to the next, resulting in continuous change" (p. 2). So, despite its way of managing the dialectical forces, a family will never be able to live outside of its own contradictions. At best, members can be like the unicyclist and pay close attention to avoid unnecessary falls.

❖ INTERFACE OF CULTURE AND
DIALECTICAL MANAGEMENT PATTERNS

In addition to having to manage the tensions inherent within family life, family members must face the demands of the social context in which they live. A family must manage the competing demands of its members, but it must also incorporate the expectations of culture into its self-definition and expression. The notion of family values, for example, as defined by some, implies that to be a real family, one must adhere to certain cultural values. Thus, according to Coontz (2000), "Almost every known society has had a legally, economically, and culturally privileged family form that confers significant advantages on those who live within it even if those advantages are not evenly distributed or are accompanied by high costs for certain family members" (p. 286). Families must assert autonomy and connection or stability and change not only to themselves but also express that beingness to others. Families regulate their access to the world "out there" by controlling their exchanges outside of themselves. Thus, restricted access across boundaries, such as limiting the family members' media exposure or not allowing them to participate in a popular social event, may enhance a family's autonomy from the culture and also be used to maintain stability.

Compared with other families and cultures, every family evolves as unique in some ways and conformist in others. In her article, "Communication as the Interface Between Couples and Culture," Montgomery (1992b) discusses how couples may also use their improvisational praxical patterns to cope with the demands of the larger society.

> *Families regulate their access to the world "out there" by controlling their exchanges outside of themselves.*

For example, the selection process that repeatedly stresses one polarity may be used when a family chooses to be so autonomous and stable that it becomes alienated from its culture as a way to avoid change and outside influence. Or, conversely, a family that is highly integrated into the culture, enacting the requirements of its social position, may ignore its unique needs. In the family that opts for selection as its management strategy, a family member's expression of individuality would threaten the family's desire to be socially appropriate, and the family would suppress such expression. The separation process, by which a family attempts to disconnect polar tensions in a given time or place, is also evident in its management of cultural demands. For example, society itself exhibits times of greater conformity and times of greater individuality. Historians even consider times of extreme conformity, as exhibited in the 1950s, to be anomalies. As Coontz (2000) says, "The 1950's family was atypical even for the 20th Century" (p. 288). Thus, compared to the 1960s, which we consider a time of expressing individualism, families were only relatively different in terms of marriage rates, working mothers, and parental involvement.

> *Although a couple may choose to take a more unique approach to marriage, the pressures of society will still provide the baseline against which we define the couple's uniqueness.*

Typically, higher connection to the culture marks relationship beginnings and endings. Weddings, births, divorces, and funerals can involve a considerable number of social expectations that may or may not adhere to personal preferences. Although a couple may choose to take a more unique approach to marriage, the pressures of society will still provide the baseline against which we define the couple's uniqueness.

In managing its relationship to the larger culture, a family may opt for neutralization or moderation between its unique needs and those societal expectations that surround it. This happy medium approach would allow for some conformity and some expression of uniqueness. A couple may be unique in that they have a commuter marriage in which their employment requires them to reside in different geographical areas, but they may maintain their fidelity to each other as the society dictates them to do. Thus, they stray from social norms to a degree, while also adhering to them in some ways.

The moderate position, however, is relative to the dictates of a given culture. What may be moderate in an urban area could be considered radical in a rural area. Furthermore, what we consider moderate in a society will change and fluctuate over time. Thus, neutralization is a temporary solution to managing competing demands of society and family life.

Reformulation, in which polarity is transcended, may also be used as a way to negotiate cultural demands on family life. A family

> *What we consider moderate in a society will change and fluctuate over time.*

may be so intent on conforming to every societal rule that it stands out from the norm; the family's extreme conformity makes them unique. A social situation can be redefined or reframed so that its initial appearance is overlooked in favor of a deeper meaning. Because social norms change over time and place, the meaning of the reformulation will eventually become irrelevant; hence, the contradiction, like appetite, may be temporarily sated but never permanently satisfied.

The options for contradiction between family and culture and within families are endless. Although we recognize that autonomy/connection and stability/change are primary dialectical forces in family life, there is vast potential for describing other contradictions. Rawlins (1992) classifies these contradictions as either contextual or interactional. He distinguishes the negotiation of tensions between interpersonal relationships and

> *Although we recognize that autonomy/connection and stability/change are primary dialectical forces in family life, there is vast potential for describing other contradictions.*

culture (contextual dialectics) from those within interpersonal relationships (interactional dialectics). His discussion is based on the study of friendship, but it seems equally applicable to the study of family life. In the section that follows, we examine the concepts of contextual and interactional dialectics.

❖ DIALECTICAL CLASSIFICATION: CONTEXT AND INTERACTION

As previously mentioned, dialectical tensions are numerous and options for classification wide open for study and speculation. Rawlins's (1992) version of the dialectical perspective, which he has applied extensively to the study of friendship, considers how friends attempt "to manage strategically the incompatible requirements of their relationship" as well as how they manage friendship "vis-à-vis other social spheres, such as family and work settings, and larger cultural orders" (p. 8). The latter, contextual dialectics, derives "from the place of friendship in the prevailing social order of American culture" (p. 9). The former, interactional dialectics, focuses on "the relationships among self's and other's behaviors and the meanings self and others assign to those behaviors" (p. 15).

Contextual Dialectics

Extending the notion that couples interface through communication with the larger culture, creating the paradox that intimacy is, in part, socially defined, the concept of contextual dialectics outlines two specific tensions: the dialectic of the private and the public, and the dialectic of the ideal and the real. Each of these is an elaboration on the ways in which cultural norms, expectations, and prescriptions, which are received via prior relational experience, interpersonal channels, and the media, "frame and permeate interaction within specific" relationships (Rawlins, 1992, p. 9). In addition to responding to cultural norms, families need to revise their responses and continually adapt to the changing nature of these norms.

Private Versus Public

The private/public dialectic, as applied to family life, refers to the contradictory pulls between the inner and outer worlds. Laws necessarily govern families—we legally define right and wrong. For example, prior to the 1950s, the notion of spouse abuse or child abuse was nonexistent. We considered the family's choices behind closed doors, especially the choices of the male head of the household, to be their own business.

Early accounts of child abuse in the 1960s attributed such behavior to pathology, and spousal abuse was within the norm as long as the abuse did not exceed the "rule of thumb."

> *The private/public dialectic, as applied to family life, refers to the contradictory pulls between the inner and outer worlds.*

Beginning in the 1970s and snowballing into the 1980s and 1990s, we have drastically reformulated our notions of what is normal regarding abuse, and we've passed laws to prevent and punish the abusers. Today, in fact, we recognize that "the violent marriage is basically engaged in a power struggle" (Gottman & Notarius, 2000, p. 936).

Another example of public/private regulation of family life through the law is in the area of homosexual rights. In this instance, what society rules as illegal—that is, the rights of same-sex partners and their families—we now challenge and question. As of this writing, the state of Vermont has become the first state to grant legal privileges similar to marriage to same-sex partners under the domain of civil union. Again, then, the notion of conforming to public expectations is at best a temporary solution to the public/private dialectic.

The public/private dialectic in family life must also be managed with respect to role expectations. Social prescriptions abound for husbands, wives, daughters, sons, sisters, brothers, mothers, fathers, and other blood relatives. Of course, expectations can be contradictory depending on the chronotopical arrangements of the situation. In one part of the world, a culture may expect a wife to act submissively, whereas another culture may expect a wife's assertiveness. The conflict of such expectations is especially evident in multicultural families. The expectations family members have for each other may also be contradictory based on previous experience or media exposure. "Big boys don't cry" may be a norm adopted by one parent and rejected by another, in which case the competition of the private and public becomes an interpersonal challenge.

While raising children, the teaching of public/private is paramount to socialization. Behavior regarding sexuality, for example, must be managed along private and public lines. As a child ages, behaviors that were once acceptable in public (e.g., nudity) become unacceptable

> *Social prescriptions abound for husbands, wives, daughters, sons, sisters, brothers, mothers, fathers, and other blood relatives.*

and even subject to a violation of law. Just where the line between public and private crosses, however, is ever-changing and difficult to determine.

Recently, a mother was arrested for having nude photos of her eight-year-old daughter processed. To her, the photos were akin to nude baby photos and innocent of any pornographic meaning. To the law, however, her behavior was considered to be in violation of public standards and abusive. It is likely that in another time and place, her behavior would have gone unquestioned.

The teaching of sexuality through public education also raises issues of family life and the public/private dialectic. Parents, educators, and administrators are forever arguing over whose job it is to socialize children about sexuality. Because we consider sexuality a private domain, some feel that it should not be publicly taught. But because the impact of not providing adequate sex education affects the culture at large (e.g., through teen pregnancies and AIDS), educators may feel they have not only the right but the obligation to bring this private matter into the public realm.

Although numerous examples of the public/private contradiction exist in family life, families have choices in terms of how they manage these tensions. As with competing demands

> *A celebrity family might manage the dialectic through separation, by which they are public at some times, such as during ceremonies, but private during other times, such as family vacations.*

for stability and change and for autonomy and connection, the choices may result in patterns of selection, separation, neutralization, and reformulation. A family using selection, for example, may choose to keep a high degree of privacy even though they are in the public eye. While President Clinton and his wife were raising their young daughter in the White House, they maintained strict privacy for their daughter when reporters were concerned. A celebrity family might manage the dialectic through separation, by which they are public at some times, such as during ceremonies, but private during other times, such as family vacations. Some may opt for neutralization, compromising their need for privacy with the public's desire to know about their personal life;

in this case, families may take reporters along on a trip but limit their access to the families' activities. The reformulation of the private/public dialectic may result in reframing an event, such as a televised wedding, as intimately public, creating a transcendent category to manage the contradiction. Maintaining privacy, whether a family is directly or more indirectly in the public eye, requires an ongoing dialectical management.

Ideal Versus Real

In addition to responding to the private/public dilemma, pressures of the ideal and the real also influence families. Ideals tend to arise from cultural expectations, whereas the "real" is that which actually occurs in families. Speaking about friendship, Rawlins (1992, p. 11) states that "the interplay between the abstract ideals and expectations often associated with friendship and the nettlesome realities or unexpected rewards of actual communication" creates this dialectic.

In application to the family, it is easy to see how ideals about family life and experienced realities exist in a dynamic interplay. Ideals often go unstated and may even remain out of our awareness, yet they can still damage a family when the ideals are unrealistic.

> The dialectic of the ideal and the real is that it is very much alive and influential in family life, often without the family's awareness.

For example, studies on males who batter find a marked tendency for these males to hold outdated and restrictive gender expectations of their female partners. They expect their "ideal spouse" to be passive and caretaking. When the spouses of these men cannot meet the unrealistic expectations the men hold, in part because they may be impossible to meet, the men blame their female partners and respond with abuse (Sabourin, 1996).

We can also argue that abstract, idealized notions about family life contribute to the family's dissolution through divorce or abandonment. A sur-

> *Ideals often go unstated and may even remain out of our awareness, yet they can still damage a family when the ideals are unrealistic.*

vey of student posters depicting the "ideal" and "real" elements of marriage, for example, showed that the ideal is held up as desirable and the real as undesir-able (Sabourin, 1999). Images associated with ideal marriages, for example, include flowers, lingerie, travel to exotic islands, fitness, and overall happiness, whereas images associated with real marriages emerge as burnt dinners, angry spouses, lack of money, boredom, and general unhappiness. Posited as a dichotomy, the ideal stands out as that which is easy and pleasant and the real as anything unpleasant or challenging. If family members hope to achieve the bliss of the idealized family, it may be easy to feel that reality is better "out there," and, thus, jump ship to a new partner. Couples working on issues of sexuality often think it would be easier to change partners than to change their own behaviors. The ideals for self or partner may create an insatiable desire to find a better life with someone else. To the extent that partners do not recognize expectations as abstract ideals, not real options, however, they may continue to discard marriage and family life in the search for something that does not exist.

Perhaps altering the associations held about the real family would enable more satisfaction for family members. As Rawlins (1992) explains, "A dialectical conception maintains that any social formation is revealed through and constituted by the end-

> *The extent and content of chosen ideals and realities will vary across time and space.*

less interweaving of idealistic and realistic factors" (p. 14). Such an integration, managed through separation or neutralization patterns, would allow for the reality of family life to be accepted along with the ideals to some extent. The extent and content of chosen ideals and realities will, of course, vary across time and space.

During relationship development, a couple may experience times of separation, in which they focus only on the ideals of marriage. We sometimes call this the "honeymoon period." At other times, the couple may compromise and accept a behavior that is not ideal, such as messiness, in recognition that an ideal behavior, such as reliability, counters the effect. In fact, we can portray the development of marriage as selection: first of the ideal during the honeymoon and then of the real, where disillusionment may set in. A later stage of marriage, acceptance, incorporates both abstract ideals and marital realities and may even reframe the less-than-ideal qualities as making the marriage rich in soulfulness. What is an endearing quality in courtship may very well become an annoyance at later times in the family. The carefree nature of a person may be initially attractive but become impractical and frustrating when the couple is raising children.

> *What is an endearing quality in courtship may become an annoyance at later times in the family.*

The point to remember about the dialectic of the ideal and the real is that it is very much alive and influential in family life, often without the family's awareness. As a family identifies and discards mismatched ideals, it may find that its own reality is actually not so one-sidedly negative. Making peace with reality while maintaining standards of import to family members can be, at least momentarily, achieved through dialectical management. Because families must live with both the ideal and the real, however, they can never ultimately resolve the tension between the two. In addition to working out a relationship between the culture and themselves through contextual dialectics, families must also negotiate relationships among themselves. The negotiation of relational contradictions is classified by Rawlins (1992) as interactional dialectics.

Interactional Dialectics

In his study of friendship, Rawlins (1992) identified four specific interactional dialectics:

1. independence and dependence

2. affection and instrumentality

3. judgment and acceptance

4. expressiveness and protectiveness.

These dialectical principles organize and compose "ongoing challenges and antagonistic choices in the practical management of communication sustaining friendship" (p. 15).

Although the character of friendship is certainly distinctive from the character of family, especially in that friendship tends to be a more voluntary arrangement whereas family is often nonvolitional, the application of these four principles can illuminate the dialectical nature of family interactions.

Independence Versus Dependence

Similar to the autonomy/connection dialectic, families must manage the contradictory demands for independence and dependence. In every relationship, there is both a desire for freedom and a contrasting desire for connection. In working out the competing forces of independence and dependence, families may rely on the patterns of selection, separation, neutralization, and reformulation to achieve a temporary resolution. A family that selects independence over dependence, for example, may

> *In every relationship, there is both a desire for freedom and a contrasting desire for connection.*

consider any sign of neediness as too demanding. Conversely, a family that selects dependence may experience interactional bids for autonomy as threatening to the family's values of closeness and togetherness. By ignoring either pole for any length of time, a family denies the persistent nature of its simultaneous demands for both dependence and independence.

Affection Versus Instrumentality

When a family is in the process of creating meaning—which is all of the time—it assigns, either knowingly or not, values to members' behaviors. The competing demands of affection and instrumentality challenge a family's definitional process. To be affectionate indicates pure liking or pure caring without alternative motivations; instrumentality, on the other hand, may mean that members enact behaviors for some payoff or reward that is external to the behavior itself. The affection, therefore, is an end in itself whereas the instrumentality is but a means to an end.

Cultural variations abound in terms of what is and is not an appropriate expression of either affection or instrumentality. In some cultures, marriage is based on affection, whereas, in others, it is based on instrumental values. In the U.S., if a young, attractive male or female becomes attracted to an older, wealthy potential partner, we question his or her motives as being instrumental or opportunistic. We expect marriage to be based on affection, which means a couple may be unprepared for the work of marriage and family life. By ignoring one polarity for another (i.e., by using selection), a family will be limited in their accomplishment of the full range of family life needs, which includes expressions of both instrumentalism and affection.

Some families may opt to manage the competing demands via separation, either topically or temporally. A topical separation means that the family deals with tensions according to content. For example, family members may opt at times to use

> *We expect marriage to be based on affection, which means a couple may be unprepared for the work of marriage and family life.*

gift-giving for instrumental purposes, such as to obtain forgiveness, and at other times, to give gifts to express affection. A temporal selection, on the other hand, separates the tensions in time. Family members may relate instrumentally to each other during a busy workweek so that they can get everything done. On the weekends, the same family may play together using unstructured time.

Some couples may neutralize the need for affection and instrumentality by seeking a compromise. They might decide that completing housework with each other gives them a chance to get some work done and to express some affection at the same time. The reformulation of affection and instrumentality such as "I work long hours to show I love you" may satisfy the competing demands for a given time, but like other strategies, it will not be a permanent resolution.

Judgment Versus Acceptance

The dialectic of judgment and acceptance reflects the evaluative quality of communication. At the same time that interaction can serve to validate one's self-concept (acceptance), it can also serve to criticize (judge). As Rawlins (1992, p. 20) explains, "It is difficult to experience another person's reactions to self as neutral." As such, interaction is fraught with the potential for ambiguity. The assignment of negotiated meaning takes place between the competing forces of judgment and acceptance in family life as well as in friendship. Family members walk the line with each other between accepting and judging every moment of the day, which is why the process of negotiating meaning becomes so critical to family development.

In his landmark study of the transition to parenthood, Stamp (1994) found that "couples must decide which differences in technique are unimportant enough to be left alone and which issues are sufficiently critical to discuss" (p. 103). A family in the habit of managing the contradictory forces through selection, for example, may remain critical in their interactions, foregoing acceptance as unnecessary. Living with such a pattern will undoubtedly affect family members' assignment of meaning outside as well as inside the household and could create negative self- and worldviews. A family may also be constantly accepting of each other, allowing no critical judgment. Here again, the tension is denied but cannot be overcome.

Family members walk the line with each other between accepting and judging every moment of the day, which is why the process of negotiating meaning becomes so critical to family development.

Separation may be used to allow for acceptance and judgment in different times and places. Some families may criticize only in private and be accepting in public. Topically, a family may develop a rule to never criticize another member's physical appearance but to allow criticism of a member's behavior. The family that neutralizes could compromise the competition between judging and accepting through strategically ambiguous remarks and behaviors that offer conditional acceptance (e.g., a parent crediting a child for cleaning her room, before the parent cleans it again the "right" way).

A reformulation of this same tension might reframe criticism as confirming "since it communicates that a person is important enough to judge" (Rawlins, 1992, p. 20). Through praxical improvisation, the tension between judging and accepting can be managed but never fully resolved.

The potential for family members to consider a given response as either judging or accepting will be heavily contextualized by previous interactions. When we try to determine whether family members intended to be critical or accepting, we may overlook the reality that the

> *When we try to determine whether family members intended to be critical or accepting, we may overlook the reality that the response can be both.*

response can be both. This contradictory force contributes to the challenge of family life and helps to explain the impact that assignment of meaning has on the family's construction of reality.

Expressiveness Versus Protectiveness

The impulse to be open with family members must be balanced with the impulse to be closed. Thus, the dialectic of expression and protection, initially discussed by Rawlins (1992) with respect to friendships, is also relevant to family life. According to Rawlins, "The apt management of this dialectical principle constitutes a reflexive challenge" (p. 22). For example, in his study of couples' interactions in the transition to parenthood, Stamp (1994) found that "an overuse of openness or involvement may tend toward enmeshment (a family interaction style with inappropriately diffuse boundaries) while too much restraint may lead toward disengagement (a family interaction style with inappropriately rigid boundaries)" (p. 104). To avoid being hurt and vulnerable to others, families may tend to select protectiveness as their style of relating. In so doing, they prevent themselves from experiencing the trust and validation that can develop from expressiveness.

On the other hand, family members who are undiscerning in their expressiveness, never opting to be closed, may also damage their relationships. Studies of self-disclosure, for example, show that when spouses select constant openness, expressing all negative and positive feelings about self and other, marital satisfaction decreases. As Stamp (1994) found, "Increased communication by itself provides no guarantee that couples will have greater marital satisfaction" (p. 108). Thus, selection of total openness or closedness does not satisfy the dilemma of the need to manage both.

Through separation, a family may deal with the tension of being both expressive and protective with boundaries; for example, it is okay to be expressive about political beliefs and opinions but protective when expressing personal feelings about family members. The neutralization of expression and protection would allow for some, but not too much, openness and intimacy. A threshold of openness might be reached during disclosure that is deemed too personal; a teen could describe to a parent that he is sexually active but not describe his behavior in greater detail. Veiled comments may suggest some protectiveness but also some expressiveness. To reformulate expressiveness and protectiveness, a family may decide that total openness really is protective of family identity and thus may come to see expression as protection.

> *A dialectical view embraces the many contradictions attendant on family life.*

The interactional dialectics focus on the ways in which family members must constantly manage contradictory impulses as they make their way through life. Whereas the contextual dialectics—private and public, and real and ideal—emphasize the ways in which families work out their relationships in conjunction with culture, interactional dialectics emphasize how the inner world of the family is dealt with on an ongoing basis.

A dialectical view embraces the many contradictions attendant on family life. Rather than suggesting that a given family should strive for a set of prescribed behaviors and meanings, this perspective describes how they actually deal with family life.

As we recognize the diversity of today's families, dialectics remains open to the diverse possibilities as they emerge in our culture. Indeed, the dialectical perspective defines family as a mass of contradictions and validates each form as real.

2

Defining the
Contemporary Family

Wwhat is a real family? Ultimately, the answer will depend on the criteria used to define *family*. Researchers who define family are starting to recognize that "contrary to established theories of family life as based on obligations among particular members to fulfill unique functions, families are now based on more voluntary ties, choices, and needs" (Allen, Blieszner, & Roberto, 2000, p. 913). This means that the definitions of family may reflect a variety of criteria with varying levels of consistency. Furthermore, we often assume these criteria rather than stipulate them overtly, which means we cannot compare results. Even worse, we may be unaware of the criteria that we use. In this book, the criteria I use to define contemporary families stress their cultural and structural diversity. Before we consider these criteria, let us review some definitions of family and the assumptions on which they are based.

❖ DEFINING THE FAMILY

What is a family? Does everyone mean the same thing when they use the term? Do scholars? Politicians? Religious leaders? Social workers? Family members? There are many ways to approach the task of definition. For instance, some definitions attempt to describe the who, what, when, where, why, and how of the nature of the family in order to provide some boundaries and to articulate who is "out" and who is "in." According to Bedford and Blieszner (1997),

> A family is a set of relationships determined by biology, adoption, marriage, and in some societies, social designation, and existing even in the absence of contact or affective involvement, and, in some cases, even after the death of certain members (p. 526).

In addition to social scientific definitions of family, which often imply legal relationships, biological relationships, or both, we should consider some commonsense notions. These models rely on assumptions of social construction. A social construction approach to defining the family starts with the idea that the family is the "known" family and that this "known" family is perpetuated through jointly told stories and symbolic metaphors. Jorgenson (1989) asks, "Where is the 'family' in family communication?" The answer? The family is *in* their communication. In other words, family is "a system of relations that comes about as individuals define those relations in their everyday communications with another" (p. 28). The family structure itself, whether the family is nuclear, blended, single-parent, or extended, is just the site for communication, not the constructed reality.

From this view, what constitutes the family is its communication, which is reflected in its relational patterns. This means that, in addition to legal criteria, relational qualities can define the family. Thus, while the social construction approach to defining a family contributes to our understanding of how family is constituted through communica-

> *The definitions of family may reflect a variety of criteria with varying levels of consistency.*

tion and not just biological and legal connections, we can still go further.

What else is there to a family besides blood ties and relationship connections? From a functional view, the family is an agent of socialization, performing the tasks necessary to develop children and citizens. Taken together, then, these three definitions of family provide a basis for our building a more complete picture of family identification.

Another way to define family is through a set of criteria from which our society and culture make choices. Fitzpatrick and Wamboldt (1990) propose that the criteria for defining the family can be multiple and conflicting and that existing narrow definitions may be

> *The family is an agent of socialization, performing the tasks necessary to develop children and citizens.*

thinly veiled political and ideological statements rather than scientifically neutral facts. For example, same-sex couples may work toward gaining the legal recognition of their relationships that is afforded heterosexual citizens through marriage. Opponents to same-sex marriage may define a real family as a heterosexual woman, a heterosexual man, and any biological children born to them through legal marriage. To grant gays and lesbians the same legal right to marry would undermine the family as these opponents define it.

As this example illustrates, *family* is in the eye of the beholder. And beholders include scholars and government officials. Accordingly, it becomes the task of those who study families "to ask individuals to indicate who is in their family, rather than making a priori assumptions" (Allen, Blieszner, & Roberto, 2000, p. 913). Defining family is not as simple as either/or: either you're related by blood and, therefore, family or you're not. When we follow a more dialectical approach that the family is "both/and," we mean that the family can meet any and all of these criteria and be physiologically related, functionally related, and emotionally related.

Family life is both stable and changing. For the sake of distributing welfare checks and marriage licenses,

> *Family is in the eye of the beholder.*

officials need a more objective way to determine who is family. As Teachman, Tedrow, and Crowder (2000) explain, those who study and work with families officially are often "forced by our need for comparable, high quality data to make use of official statistics that all assume a legal definition of marriage and the family" (p. 1234).

This was recently evident after the terrorist attacks on September 11 in New York City, when surviving partners of same-sex relationships struggled to be recognized as family when they attempted to claim the same

> *Family life is both stable and changing.*

rights awarded to survivors of legally defined families. This is but one example of how we must embrace a more subjective criteria if we're to live in today's real world.

What is a family? A domain of activities, a quality of experience, and a metaphor. The family as a bounded system will include some individuals and exclude others. The resulting group of people that is included will be determined by the criteria used to select them. A government agent working in social welfare may find that the physiological relationships are paramount. To a newly divorced single mom, the emotional relation may be most important. Thus, the meaning of family will depend on the purpose and position of the person(s) defining it. No one meaning is the *true* meaning, but rather, the relevant meaning for that particular time and place.

❖ CRITERIA FOR DEFINING FAMILY

A good starting place for defining the family—in other words, a redefinition that recognizes structural diversity—is to specify optional rules or criteria. Based on the definitional issues we've just discussed, it seems that we use three specific criteria, either alone or in combination, to define the family. When family membership is determined by biological relations and/or law, the criterion is physical; when membership is determined by the tasks that are performed, the criteria is function; and when family is defined by the quality of its relationships, the criterion is interactional (Fitzpatrick & Wamboldt, 1990).

> *What is a family?*
> *A domain of activities, a quality of experience, and a metaphor.*

The physical family includes all those people who are related by blood ties or law. Furthermore, "The census defines a family as 'a group of two persons or more (one of whom is a householder) related by birth, marriage, or adoption and residing together.' A married couple [is] defined as a 'husband and wife enumerated as members of the same household'" (Teachman, Tedrow, & Crowder, 2000, pp. 1234–1235). Biological parents, aunts, uncles, cousins, and grandparents are

> *Whether or not any of these relatives perform any functional role, and even if they have not spoken for 20 years, we consider them family.*

obvious choices for this category of family. Relatives by law, that is, husbands and wives and in-laws, are also included as physical family. Whether or not any of these relatives perform any functional role, and even if they have not spoken for 20 years, we consider them family.

The Physical Criterion

In Research and for Social Programs

Many definitions of family rely on the physical criterion to set the boundaries. Sometimes researchers use this criterion because it is more fixed and objective than either functional or interactional criteria. A blood relation is always a blood relation—biology does not change. Whether a given individual is personally close or even known to other family members, circumstances that are subject to change, does not enter into the definition. Researchers can easily access legal documents to specify biological relations, which in turn enables a set and objective definition of the family to be studied. If, rather than simply assuming the biological criterion, researchers had to ask their subjects who they considered to be family and why, research would require a lot more time and money than most researchers have. So, partly for the sake of convenience and objectivity, scholars commonly use the physical criterion. For similar reasons, social service agencies supported by the government use the biological or physically related criterion to define *family*.

Politics and Religion

Politicians, religious leaders, and ordinary laypeople who attempt to define the family also use the physical criterion, but for different reasons. Politicians who consider the real family to be biologically related may do so to espouse a set of values that may be agreeable to their constituents. Conservative politicians have been very vocal about issues of "family values," by which they usually mean (although they probably don't directly state it) intact, nuclear families. When Dan Quayle was vice president, he openly criticized Murphy Brown, a television show character, for portraying a single woman choosing to have a baby outside of marriage. This particular arrangement, according to his notion of family values, disqualified the character and her baby from *real family* status.

Similarly, religious agendas supporting a particular moral stance center on the physical criterion of families, using either biology or law to determine who is and who is not a real family.

Even laypeople, who have the most intimate knowledge of who they consider to be part of their families, who they exclude, and why, will often feel oblig-

> *Politicians who consider the real family to be biologically related may do so to espouse a set of values that may be agreeable to their constituents.*

ated to automatically count all blood or legal kin as family. Despite the lack of a functional or an interactional relationship, the idea that "blood is thicker than water" is often applied even among those with no political or religious agenda. However, "if families are not objectively real, then they too must be viewed as social arrangements that persons construct and then define as families" (Scanzoni & Marsiglio, 1993, p. 109). As a result, "ties of blood and/or marriage do not guarantee a sense of we-ness" (Scanzoni & Marsiglio, 1993, p. 113).

The Functional Criterion

The family is complex. And as Bernardes (1993) states, "Not only is family life varied and complex, but this variation and complexity is very difficult to study" (p. 41). Although many consider the physical criterion to be a necessary one, it is not always sufficient to account for who is bound into the family. The functional criterion, which is implied in many definitions of family, can also be used to provide a more complete understanding of family boundaries. Using this criterion, people are family members if they perform certain socialization functions. In our society, these include educating children, teaching them to be good citizens, and providing food, clothing, and shelter and attending to medical needs. The family is responsible for providing children with an education, taking care of their physical well being, and teaching them right from wrong. While both family and school can teach children about sexuality, evolution, and morality, debates abound between parents and educators about the content and approach to be taken. Whereas parents often do not want educators to take on this role, teachers may feel that parents do not always do an adequate job.

When it comes to family functions, it is useful to consider a both/and approach, rather than an either/or one, to describe what families actually do instead of what they are expected to do. As an example, because parents alone or teachers alone may not adequately teach sex education, the both/and dialectical approach suggests that both can do it together. Thus, when it comes to defining the family on the basis of functional criterion, we cannot assume that if someone performs a given function or fails to perform a given function, he or she will be counted as a family member. The functional criterion is an important one nonetheless, and, when combined with the criteria for physical relationships, provides a more profound understanding of how family can be defined.

The Interactional Criterion

The interactional criterion expresses the nature of the family's interpersonal climate, describing the quality of the relationships between family members. Within a given family, we-ness is "a variable measuring the degree to which persons feel a part of others ('I matter, I'm impor- tant') and the degree to which persons per- ceive that others feel a

> *When it comes to family functions, it is useful to consider a both/and approach, rather than an either/or one, to describe what families actually do instead of what they are expected to do.*

part of them" (Scanzoni & Marsiglio, 1993, pp. 113–114). We might consider someone as family because that person is sup- portive and nurturing. The level of intimacy between family members is an important quality that distinguishes them from nonfamily. According to this criterion, family members reveal commitment to each other through their interactions, and they are important contributors to each others' identity formations. Because of this, the family influence on self-concept has the potential to be both far-reaching and long-lasting.

The interactional qualities in the family context differ system- atically from those in other contexts, such as organizations and

> *Family is a unique context for study because its influence has great longevity.*

small groups (Yerby, Buerkel-Rothfuss, & Bochner, 1995). Family membership is considered to be nonvolitional, unlike membership in other groups; hence, whether the relationship is close or distant, it cannot be dissolved. Also, the family of origin critically affects how its members form concepts about themselves. The evolution of the self is determined to some degree by the quality of relation- ships with other family members. Family is a unique context for study because its influence has great longevity. Long after people have moved away from family members geographically, they still feel psychologically and emotionally connected to them.

The level of commitment and intimacy is another quality that distinguishes family membership from that in other organizations or groups. Most of us expect our family members to stick together and by us through thick and thin. The traditional marriage vows pledge couples to stay together through sickness and health, under all conditions. Families are expected to maintain their commitment no matter what happens.

The notion of qualitative purpose is another distinguishing factor for defining the family. *Qualitative purpose* means that a family is concerned with its members' emotional needs and with the quality of their lives rather than with the bottom line of productivity, a primary concern for organizations and other groups. In family life, people are of primary importance. Because a family also requires

> *Unlike a business in which interpersonal relations are considered secondary to getting the work done, the family needs to get its work done in a way that is sensitive to interpersonal relationships.*

life-sustaining functions, some work must be done. What distinguishes a family from other contexts is its simultaneous orientation: Families must accomplish tasks and, at the same time, respect the interpersonal quality of their relationships. They must eat, clothe themselves, and house themselves, all of which require money, which means provision of an income through some nonfamily efforts. Unlike a business in which interpersonal relations are considered secondary to getting the work done, the family needs to get its work done in a way that is sensitive to interpersonal relationships.

As this discussion indicates, the interactional criterion helps explain the relational quality of family life. Indeed, it is the management of the dialectical tension between autonomy and connection that guides much of family interaction. Because of this, it is critical that researchers not ignore the qualitative nature of family life by overemphasizing its physical and/or functional natures. Often times, when laypeople are asked why they consider someone to be family, they will reflect on the quality of experience that they associate with family life. Many expect and desire that quality to be dominated by the support and closeness polarity of the autonomy/connection dialectic. But if we use only the interactional criterion to distinguish who is in and who is not in the family, we will be misled. The interactional criterion is crucial in that it contributes to a more holistic definition of family, but it is not a sufficient criterion to account for the complexity of boundaries.

Family definition is complex and dynamic. By using all three criteria, some combination, or just one, we have choices of how we conceive family to be. What is important for the study of family life, then, is not necessarily to use these specific criteria to define families, but to be explicit about whatever criteria we use, both to subjects engaged in research and consumers of the written research product.

Trost (1993), noting that "the term *family* is traditionally referred to as a social group" consisting of dyads, hopes that researchers "might come to an agreement of what sort of 'language' to use when distinguishing one variety of family from another" (pp. 92–93). The language that she proposes relies on the dyadic unit so that we can trace the changes through "parental separation, parental recohabitation, and remarriage" that are likely to occur (p. 103). The varieties of families that are described, then, would be "analyzed and compared with the approach of dyads within dyads," in which each family member can be counted as a part of one or more families (p. 102).

If researchers ask subjects to list family members, they must be clear about the criteria they're using. Assumed criteria may lead to confusing results, especially if subjects' definitions and researchers' definitions are inconsistent.

In Chapter 3, we'll look at structural diversity in family life. We will see how the definition of family emerges from the assignment of the physical, functional, and/or interactional criteria, and we will consider the differences and similarities of viable family structures.

3

The Contemporary Family

Structural Diversity

❖ COMMON FAMILY STRUCTURES

It has been common practice to assume that structure is destiny when it comes to predicting the quality of family life because, as Allen and Farnsworth (1993) claim, the knowledge base on which family studies rest is biased toward "white, middle-class, heterosexual, married adults with children" (p. 352). They go on to say that "this family structure, known as the bench-mark family, is the standard against which all other families are judged" (p. 352). In the hierarchy of family structures, we tend to place the nuclear family ahead of all other configurations. "In functionalist thought, certain structures become institutionalized, that is, culturally legitimated. Variations on those structures are labeled as deviant" (Scanzoni & Marsiglio, 1993, p. 106). The nuclear family has become the standard. The blended family, with at least one biological parent and one stepparent in the formula, comes second. The single-parent family structure comes last in the hierarchy, especially if headed by an unwed mother.

Given this hierarchy, most families are not destined to be successful because nuclear families, with a biological mother and a biological father, are statistically a minority, whereas blended and single-parent families are in the majority: an *increasing* majority. In fact, for women born between 1970 and 1974, "40% of white women and 46% of African American women had experienced more than one living arrangement while growing up" (Teachman, Tedrow, & Crowder, 2000, p. 1240). Among the youngest women of this group, across race, 25% had lived in *three or more childhood arrangements*. It is thought, then, that the experience of change for children, "beyond any effect associated with experiencing a single-parent family, is also detrimental to the well-being of children" (Teachman, Tedrow, & Crowder, 2000, p. 1240). It is the degree of change, which can be more extreme or less extreme depending on individual family circumstances, and not just the resultant structure that accounts for children's difficulties in the nonnuclear structure.

> *In the hierarchy of family structures, we tend to place the nuclear family ahead of all other configurations.*

This means that a dialectical management approach, which heavily emphasizes the ways in which families express the tensions between stability and change, can be very relevant to the study of changing family structures. From a distance, it may be easy to judge the family by its structure. But research suggests that structure alone is not a valid basis on which to predict and judge the potential for success in family life. Instead, it is more valid and fruitful to approach family structure from a descriptive stance. Dialectically, all families possess strengths and weaknesses. In fact, dialectically, a family who identifies only with its strengths may actually transform that strength into a weakness

(Charny, 1986). That being said, this chapter considers structural diversity from a descriptive, rather than prescriptive, viewpoint.

Because the contemporary family is so diverse in structure, it is likely that any given child will experience more than one parental configuration throughout his or her lifetime. "We seem to have reached

> *From a distance, it may be easy to judge the family by its structure. But research suggests that structure alone is not a valid basis on which to predict and judge the potential for success in family life.*

a dynamic structure in some countries where children can assume or presume that [their parents] will cohabit, split up, cohabit again, and then marry, divorce, recohabit, split up, recohabit, remarry, and so on" (Trost, 1993, p. 103). The standard, then, has become "a number of cohabiting relationships, a number of marriages/remarriages, and a number of separations and divorces" (p. 103). As such, structure has become more of a process than a fixed arrangement. This means that "before becoming an adult, the child will experience parental separation, parental recohabitation, and remarriage a number of times, meaning a number of stepmothers and stepfathers and real parents in different households" (p. 103).

Dialectically, structure is a source of both stability and change. Whereas we once assumed that structure would be a permanent arrangement, in the current society of the United States, structure is in flux, evolving and changing in a revolutionary way. From the dialectical stance of both/and, change

> *Because the contemporary family is so diverse in structure, it is likely that any given child will experience more than one parental configuration throughout his or her lifetime.*

precludes pure homeostasis, acting instead as a transformer of it. Change constantly interrupts stability, requiring dialectical management rather than our own sweeping judgments that change shouldn't be happening. Thus, although we may consider the composition of family structure as sacred, the empirical evidence does not support this kind of stability.

We may sometimes overestimate the impact of unique family structures on determining the quality of family life. As a great deal of research shows, a number of cultural factors can affect the quality of family life in a significant way. Economics, for example, though not unrelated to structure, plays a big role in determining the resources available to parents and children that allow for or inhibit a quality family life. To untangle the range of influence that structure and culture exert on the family, we will examine here the research on family structure. We will look at specific configurations: the nuclear family, the single-parent family, and the blended family. In a chapter that follows, we will explore another set of variables that affect family life: cultural diversity.

The Nuclear Family

> We may sometimes overestimate the impact of unique family structures on determining the quality of family life. As a great deal of research shows, a number of cultural factors can affect the quality of family life in a significant way.

When we use the term *nuclear family*, we mean the family structure of two parents, in their first marriage, and their biological children. Sometimes referred to as an "intact" family, this structure has been idealized in our culture in that, by virtue of two biological parents in their first marriage, this arrangement implies marital stability. To idealize this structure means to allocate secondary status to other structures.

In their controversial article, "Deconstructing the Essential Father," Silverstein and Auerbach (1999) challenge the notion that the biological parent, specifically the father, is necessarily the best parent to raise a child. They claim that an essentialist perspective, which exalts the nuclear structure, oversimplifies its interpretation of existing family research and "the complex relations between father presence and social problems" (p. 397). The essentialist perspective "defines mothering and fathering as distinct social roles that are not interchangeable" (p. 397). In contrast, Silverstein and Auerbach's research supports their assertion that "responsible fathering can occur within a variety of family structures" (p. 397). They conclude from their own research "that children need at least one responsible, caretaking adult who has a positive emotional connection to them and with whom they have a consistent relationship" (pp. 397-398). Furthermore, although essentialism advocates traditional family roles, some studies show that "fathers who are more involved with their children overall tend to be ones who hold nontraditional gender roles and egalitarian family role ideologies" (McLoyd, Cauce, Takeuchi, & Wilson, 2000, p. 1081).

Nonessentialists, then, reject the physical criteria for defining family and emphasize functional and interactional criteria. Hence, the essentialist and nonessentialist views differ in the criteria they use to define family and their resulting prescriptions for family life. This also suggests that the values that inform a researcher's perspective influence his or her interpretation of results. Accordingly, research that depends on the structure as a determining factor in the quality of family life overlooks the importance of cultural influence.

In their studies of families in the United States, Silverstein and Auerbach (1999) found that the least involved parents were teenage fathers, who lack financial resources, and upper-class, traditional fathers, whose wives' economic contributions are nonexistent or minimized. Hence, teen dads, "who are often undereducated and underemployed . . . cannot make a meaningful contribution to the economic security of their children"

> *The values that inform a researcher's perspective influence his or her interpretation of results. Accordingly, research that depends on the structure as a determining factor in the quality of family life overlooks the importance of cultural influence.*

(p. 401). Traditional, upper-class fathers, on the other hand, are not actively involved in parenting because they use their time to make the money to pay others to tend to their children. Furthermore, because social policy that is based on essentialist values discriminates against diverse family structures, its impact helps to determine the resources available to families. If resources are withheld from non-nuclear families, the lack of resources, rather than the family's structure per se, may reinforce the family's inherent weaknesses and undermine its potential to develop its strengths. In this way, essentialist values may be upheld and perpetuated even though they lack external validity to family life as a whole.

What scholars from a nonessentialist view of family life want is to encourage "public policy that supports the legitimacy

> *If resources are withheld from non-nuclear families, the lack of resources, rather than the family's structure per se, may reinforce the family's inherent weaknesses and undermine its potential to develop its strengths.*

of diverse family structures, rather than policy that privileges the two-parent, heterosexual, married family" (Silverstein & Auerbach, 1999, p. 399). Furthermore, in that they stress the functional nature of parenting, nonessentialists maintain that parental quality is independent of family structure.

Although a number of researchers recognize the proliferation of family structures in contemporary society, many still use assumptions from the nuclear family model "as the golden standard against which all other family configurations are compared" (Gamache, 1997, p. 41). Models of family development, for example, assume the nuclear family as the normative structure. As a result, these models assume a linear progression of development:

- courtship
- early marriage
- birth of children
- the aging of children from infancy through adolescence
- the children's greater independence through marriage, college, or career
- the subsequent retirement and death of the still-married spouses.

We consider interruptions to this pattern of development as unpredictable sources of change. However, given that most families today do not take a simple linear path in the course of their development, the model that characterizes the nuclear family inadequately expresses how all families develop. To the extent that we use the nuclear structure to determine the path of normal family development, we obscure the many variations that families actually create.

Change as a Constant

From a dialectical view, we do not experience change as a transition between stable periods of development, as suggested by the linear nuclear model, but, rather, we

> *To the extent that we use the nuclear structure to determine the path of normal family development, we obscure the many variations that families actually create.*

experience change as a constant. Instead of characterizing family life by long periods of stability (i.e., stages of courtship, early marriage, and so forth) with short periods of transition in between these stages, the dialectical view portrays family life as constant change with the potential for short periods of stability in between. Because of the need to manage dialectical forces, change will transform the family in ways that are both predictable and unpredictable. Although many families may exist in a nuclear structure at some point in time, it is likely that they will experience a variety of structures as they make their way through family life. The notion of structure, therefore, may be more meaningful when we describe its fluctuating status rather than rank it hierarchically.

The nuclear structure creates expectations not only for social agents, such as school counselors, social workers, and researchers, but also for people who actually live in families, which includes, of course, researchers and social agents. If people believe that they're second-rate because they live in single-parent or blended-family households, their potential in these families is limited. Our idealization of the nuclear family can be damaging in that it influences how researchers construct their knowledge about families and how people limit themselves as non-nuclear family members.

> *Because of the need to manage dialectical forces, change will transform the family in ways that are both predictable and unpredictable.*

In the next sections, we see that, just as the nuclear structure contains the potential for both strength and weakness, the single-parent and blended families are also viable family structures. We consider these structural variations not from a hierarchical perspective, with nuclear at the top and single-parent at the bottom, but as evolutionary configurations. In this way, we gain an appreciation for how family members adapt from one structure to the next, as they do through divorce and remarriage.

The Single-Parent Family

The contemporary family is dynamic and changing; the term *family* may refer to a variety of structures, including no legal relationships (e.g., cohabitation), voluntary social groupings (e.g., communes), adults without children, or same-sex civil unions. The contemporary family is characterized by flux; it is likely that a given structure will occur for some period of time but is unlikely to be permanent. In all families, regardless of structure, functional and interactional needs exist. In families in which there are children, these needs are met with varying degrees of effectiveness through parenting.

Parenting is a process composed of tasks, roles, rules, and rights. Individuals, couples, extended families, and institutions can fulfill parenting functions, such as nurturing and protecting children (Horowitz, 1995). In the single-parent family, the tasks, roles, rules, and rights of parenting,

> *The contemporary family is characterized by flux; it is likely that a given structure will occur for some period of time but is unlikely to be permanent.*

which, in a nuclear structure is shared by two parents, become the responsibility of one adult who may or may not be the biological parent. According to the most recent U.S. census, there are 12 million one-parent families, 10 million of which are headed by females (U.S. Census Bureau, 2000). Furthermore, McLoyd, Cauce, Takeuchi, and Wilson (2000) report that, in 1998, the percentage of single-parent homes among African Americans was 54.8% and among European Americans, 22.8%. In African American single-parent homes, the head of the household was three times as likely to be female as in European American homes.

Statistics show that single-parent homes are becoming more prevalent. Indeed, many adults and children are likely to live in a single-family structure at some point in their lives. Though single-parent families are sometimes referred to as "broken homes," they can also be studied for the ways in which they successfully manage the challenges that face them, and often, manage these challenges as effectively as nuclear families do.

> *Though single-parent families are sometimes referred to as "broken homes," they can also be studied for the ways in which they successfully manage the challenges that face them, and often, manage these challenges as effectively as nuclear families do.*

In fact, what we find to be critical in any family with children, regardless of its structure, is the formation of a nurturing and consistent attachment between a primary adult and the child (or children, as the case may be). Critical to this bonding process is the management of the aforementioned tasks, roles, rules, and rights attendant on parenting in our contemporary society. Tasks, or functions, associated with the parenting process include those that promote the child's growth from infancy (or, if adopted, from the age of custody) to early adulthood (Horowitz, 1995). This means that parents impart values, hone their children's skills, and model roles for their children. An adult of any gender, sexual orientation, age, race, religion, or socioeconomic status can effectively perform these tasks. However, the resources of time, money, communication skills, and energy can vary along with cultural factors, and all of these may affect the quality of parenting. It is not, therefore, the structure per se that determines the potential for success in child-rearing. The success of parenting will be, instead, the result of all support and guidance provided to children during their journey to adulthood.

The parent in the single-parent family is more likely than are parents with partners to suffer from responsibility overload. In a two-parent home, parents share decisions, divide tasks, and carry emotional strains on two backs instead of one. Of course, the single parent may secure help from family members, friends, and social services, yet the ultimate load of responsibility is still legally (and emotionally) the province of

> *What we find to be critical in any family with children, regardless of its structure, is the formation of a nurturing and consistent attachment between a primary adult and the child.*

one parent. As a result of this role strain, single parents are more vulnerable to burnout, which means that parenting may be less consistent than in two-parent homes where role responsibilities are shared. This does not mean, however, that this structure is inferior, only that it presents particular constraints and problems for dialectical management.

Single-parent homes can emerge from a number of circumstances. In 1991, Cargan listed the causes of single-parent homes as

- divorce (42%)
- long separation (24%)
- no marriage (27%)
- death of spouse (7%).

This means that, although we assume most are products of divorce (and hence "broken"), single-parent families can be the result of intentional choice (e.g., through adoption, artificial insemination, or nonbonded coupling). Sometimes unintentional circumstances, such as the death of a spouse or the impregnation of an unwed teenager, lead to single-parent families. It may not be the structure itself that determines the path

> *Single parents are more vulnerable to burnout, which means that parenting may be less consistent than in two-parent homes where role responsibilities are shared.*

of the child in the single-parent home; the circumstances under which the structure was formed may also have an impact on the quality of family life. Although single-parent homes have been associated with higher risk for children in terms of social and emotional outcomes, a host of factors beyond the structure contributes to the level of risk. It is the interaction of structure with other factors that influences outcomes for children.

In terms of family climate, a study conducted by Kurdeck and Fine (1993) examined the number of parenting transitions and the relationship this number had to adolescents' appraisals of family climate and parenting style. In this study, Kurdeck and Fine defined transitions thus:

No transition: the child from a nondivorced, biological family

One transition: the child in the single-parent family

Two transitions: the child with remarried parents.

As expected, those adolescents with no transitions rated family climate and parenting style more positively than others did.

In her study of children's adjustment patterns, Hetherington (1999) found that children in nondivorced but highly conflicted families and children in divorced families both exhibit similar adjustment problems. The problems most likely to occur include externalizing disorders, such as a "lack of self-regulation, low social responsibility, and cognitive agency" as well as internalizing disorders, such as social agency and self-esteem, and "difficulties in relations with parents, siblings, peers, and teachers." Although these problems are apparent in childhood, they may manifest divergently in adolescence, when children with divorced parents exhibit some unique adjustment patterns. However, Hetherington found that "the vast majority of children from divorced families eventually emerge as reasonably competent individuals who are resilient and eventually able to cope with their adverse life situations" (p. 96).

A host of factors associated with divorce can lead to problems during childhood. Taking into account life-course changes, such as the formation and dissolution of marriages, children experience "enormous change in their living arrangements which in itself can be detrimental to their well-being, especially if it is not managed effectively" (Teachman, Tedrow, & Crowder, 2000, p. 1239). Also important among these changes is the highly negative experience of economic decline that can lead to "multiple changes in residence, loss of friends, moves to poorer neighborhoods with fewer resources, inadequate schools and delinquent peer groups, lack of social support, family conflict, parental depression, inept and non-authoritative parenting, and loss or diminished contact with the non-custodial parent" (Hetherington, 1999, p. 96).

The custodial adult's parenting style is key to managing these changes. We find that authoritative parenting, which consists of warmth and a high level of monitoring, is most effective in managing these problems. As we discussed in previous chapters, the ability to manage the tension between support and control or expression and closedness is an important dialectical issue faced by families as they go through the lifestyle changes that are so common among the modern American family.

Let us consider the single-parent family that emerges from divorce. This family experiences a flood of change. Members can manage in various ways the dialectical

> *We find that authoritative parenting, which consists of warmth and a high level of monitoring, is most effective in managing these problems.*

task of maintaining a degree of stability in the midst of such change. The family may enact a separation strategy by which members attempt to keep some aspect of their family life stable while acknowledging the change. Temporally, they may decide that, on birthdays and holidays, they will act as they did pre-divorce.

Topically, they may choose to stay in the neighborhood, a constant, while they adjust to other changes. Some families neutralize the flood of change through custodial compromises in which children may live with one parent part of the week and the other parent part of the week. They may attempt selection of the contradiction, refusing to recognize anything as stable or worth maintaining in the midst of loss and change. Some families may opt to reframe the change as leading to a new kind of stability. However it manages, each family who goes through divorce faces an abundance of change in their day-to-day lives.

Another risk in single-parent families is parentification, "a type of role reversal where the child assumes roles usually considered to be parental roles" (Hetherington, 1999, p. 108). When children assume responsibility for household tasks and care of siblings, they exhibit *instrumental parentification*. When children assume the role of advisor of a needy parent or that parent's confidant, they exhibit *emotional parentification*. Studies of divorced families find that parentification occurs differently in father- and in mother-headed households. In general, mothers are more likely to place children in emotionally responsible roles, whereas fathers are more likely to expect instrumental parentification from their children. These patterns do vary somewhat, however, due to the child-parent gender configuration. Girls, for example, "encounter more emotional parentification from both mothers and fathers than do boys" (p. 109). Adolescents in both female- and male-headed households took on more tasks and responsibilities than did adolescents in nondivorced, two-parent homes. Although the consequences of parentification vary for children, with some more adversely affected than others, "children are often less cared for and more overburdened by responsibilities following divorce" (p. 112). This means that their own childhoods are interrupted and opportunities for autonomy may be slighted.

Dialectically, the process of divorce creates a paradox in which cohesion is at once increased and decreased in various family relationships. Disengagement, which is characterized by an extreme degree of autonomy, and enmeshment, which is characterized by an extreme degree of cohesion, are likely to occur simultaneously as parents let go of roles and children take them on. Marital partners once considered to be intimate, at least enough to procreate, must renegotiate a more distant relationship; children who are geographically separated from a parent to whom they were formerly close must adapt to more autonomy with that parent, while the custodial parent may require more intense closeness from the child.

As with the dialectic of stability and change, praxical patterns emerge in families as they manage the autonomy and togetherness that occur through divorce. A family who chooses selection as a management strategy may opt for total autonomy, with one parent prohibiting any contact with the other and acting as if their former structure never existed. Parents who kidnap their own children and form a new life in an unknown place are, in a sense, exhibiting selection. Separation, in which families manage contradiction either temporally or topically, occurs through family members recognizing autonomy in some times and places and togetherness in others. Visitation rights might provide specifications that the noncustodial parent and the child may be together at a certain time, maybe every Sunday. Topically, the parents may agree that they will decide together on matters relating to the children's education, while the custodial parent will make autonomous decisions about what the child wears.

To neutralize the autonomy and connection that comes through divorce, couples may opt to maintain congenial relations and may even share vacations and holidays together. In this way, they allow for more autonomy than was present in their marriage but still provide a sense of connection that is familiar to their former structure. The reformulation of autonomy and connection may take the shape of a new structure, in which the family considers itself to be a work in progress rather than a family in demise. Whatever the cause of single-parent structure—divorce, death, or choice—parents and children will face challenges that are both unique to their structure and common to all family types. To the extent that families meet these challenges with adequate resources, they can minimize the risk factors associated with this structural configuration.

Hetherington (1999) concludes that an effective solution for meeting the challenges of single-parent families created through divorce is for the parents to form "an intimate caring relationship with a new partner" (p. 114). To the extent that this relationship with a new partner leads to remarriage, the single-parent structure exists as a kind of way station between initial marriage, divorce, and remarriage. Although all single-parent families may not choose to reform as a blended family through remarriage, many do. More and more families blend together, merging children from prior marriages and giving birth to their own children. Blended families create a whole new structure and, with it, challenges and potentials unique to itself and challenges common to all family structures. In the next section, we examine blended families at length.

> *To neutralize the autonomy and connection that comes through divorce, couples may opt to maintain congenial relations and may even share vacations and holidays together.*

The Blended Family Structure

As the nuclear family declines in numbers, the blended family, or stepfamily, has become increasingly common. However, "Researchers paid little attention to stepfamilies until the 1970s, when divorce replaced bereavement as the leading precursor to remarriage" (Coleman, Ganong, & Fine, 2000, p. 1288). Furthermore, "Divorces are followed frequently by family re-formations" in which the family becomes "another structure, often a stepfamily" (Trost, 1993, p. 103). The remarriage that creates the stepfamily is also complex in its variations because "remarriage as a term encompasses several different types of relationships—both partners may be in a second or a higher-order marriage (e.g., a third or fourth marriage) or the marriage may be a remarriage for only one of the partners" (Coleman, Ganong, & Fine, 2000, p. 1289).

We estimate that nearly one in five households with married couples qualifies as a stepfamily, and we predict that this number will continue to rise (Hughes & Schroeder, 1997; Phillips, 1997). Despite its proliferation, "Assumptions from the nuclear family model permeate our view of the stepfamily" (Gamache, 1997, p. 41). The social reality for the blended family, however, is more complex than that of the nuclear family. As a result, an adequate model of stepfamily development must stress "how a stepfamily functions differently than a biological nuclear family" (Miles, 1984, p. 365).

By definition, a blended family structure contains two adults and at least one child from a previous union of either partner. This means that courtship for the

> We estimate that nearly one in five households with married couples qualifies as a stepfamily, and we predict that this number will continue to rise.

couple is not dyadic, as it is in the nuclear family, but triadic, given the presence of at least one child. According to Coleman, Ganong, and Fine (2000), when a female has children from prior relationships, a couple's "common courtship pattern is as follows: (a) male partner spends a few nights per week in the mother's household followed by (b) a brief time of full-time living together, followed by (c) remarriage" (p. 1290). The nuclear family, on the other hand, begins with a dyad, allowing for partners to concentrate on their own relationship during courtship. Most marital experts advise couples to wait to get to know each other even after marriage before bringing children into their union. This allows time to become familiar with their spousal roles before launching into the challenges of parenting. Couples who start off with children from previous unions do not have the same luxury of time but must launch immediately into parenting roles.

Even more challenging is the fact that these couples must also deal with the lingering effects of the previous union through which the stepchild was conceived. Unlike other families, "Stepfamilies are defined by the presence of a parent-child relationship that pre-dates the couple relationship" (Crosbie-Burnett & McClintic, 2000, p. 37). A blended family's pattern of development includes phases that are distinctive from those of other family structures. These phases reflect the blended family's history of loss due to the dissolution of the previous family structure, its period of reformation as a single-parent family if the previous union was a marriage, and its subsequent adjustment to a new, blended family structure.

Negative stereotypes sometimes work against the successful formation of the blended family. In their study of societal views on stepfamilies, Ganong and Coleman (1997) found two predominant patterns: (a) stepfamilies are ignored and "excluded from legal and social policy considerations, and they are often disregarded by social institutions such as schools and religious systems" (p. 85); or (b) compared to nuclear families, they are seen as deficient, dysfunctional, and problematic, "possessing mostly negative traits and characteristics" (p. 86). Families might more easily meet the challenges of blending if others looked at the potential of a blended structure rather than emphasizing its constraints. Rather than assuming only negative qualities, a more open-minded view would reveal "the rich diversity and variety" (p. 86) of ways in which blended families create their relationships. As Crosbie-Burnett and McClintic (2000) explain, "There are many types of stepfamilies, including divorced parents who remarry or cohabit, widows and widowers who are parents and who remarry or cohabit, and never married parents who marry or cohabit" (p. 37). Furthermore, new partners may be same-sex or heterosexual; children can "be residents of, or visitors to, the home"; and the families "can be of mixed race, can be of mixed culture, or can include an adopted or foster child and grandparents or other kin" (p. 37).

The blended family structure will remain uninstitutionalized as long as we measure it against the nuclear family structure. Especially in the initial phases of blending, the family members themselves are likely to use a nuclear-family map to guide them through change. And because of this map, they are likely to become disoriented or even lost.

> *Families might more easily meet the challenges of blending if others looked at the potential of a blended structure rather than emphasizing its constraints.*

Comparisons to the previous family life are unavoidable and may be especially felt between the stepparent and child. Stepfamilies may try to "recreate the nuclear family because it is familiar and simpler to deal with than the reality of stepfamily complexity and ambiguity" (Ganong & Coleman, 1997, p. 91). Furthermore, stepparents, unlike biological parents, have no clear-cut role to play in the life of their newly inherited children. The range of the stepparent relationship includes everything from a "full parent," who expects to be, and is expected to be, totally involved with the raising of the child, to a "non-parent" who delegates the role of raising the child or children to the biological parent. As such, there is less of a consensus about stepparent roles than there is about biological parent roles.

Media images of stepparents may also contribute to the negative stereotypes we associate with stepfamilies, referring to stepparents as "stepmonsters" (Ganong & Coleman, 1997, p. 91). We can trace such negative images to earlier centuries (1600–1800). During these centuries in England, the stepmother was depicted as "a figure of cruelty and evil, constantly plotting to harm her stepchildren in a myriad ways"; in France, the word *"marâtre* means both 'stepmother' and a 'cruel or harsh mother'" (Phillips, 1997, p. 12). Also, conflict between stepparents and stepchildren over resources, both material and relational, and the complications of inheritance were assumed to cause tensions between the spouses, contributing to an overall negative image. Stepchildren have also been portrayed as "children who do not belong, or whose quality of belonging is not much greater than that of orphans" (Phillips, 1997, p. 12).

Despite these negative images, the reality of blended family life can be rewarding for both children and adults. Current research identifies "positive outcomes for adults and children as the result of remarriage" (Hughes & Schroeder, 1997, p. 281). Depending on how challenges are met by both parents and children, the blended family has the potential to enhance life for its members. This indicates, then, that although the structure is complex, family members can respond in ways that effectively meet its challenges.

Challenges facing families with a blended structure include effectively managing stability and change as well as autonomy and cohesion. These dialectical forces manifest themselves uniquely in blended families. The competing forces of stability and change will require "transitional adjustments" (Hughes & Schroeder, 1997, p. 283) among stepfamily members, who must accommodate their "lack of shared history and rituals" as well as "the entry and exit of children due to visitation in several households" (p. 283). Changing family dynamics also provide challenges to autonomy and cohesion through issues of "closeness, competition for time, and the variety and complexity of the various relationships within the family" (p. 283). In addition, "Natural tensions between family members' individual development and the family's development exist in blended families," which involves a need for realignment of boundaries and individual adjustments (Crosbie-Burnett & McClintic, 2000, p. 37).

To manage these tensions, families may opt for strategies of selection, separation, neutralization, and/or reformulation.

Institutionally, schools and other social service agencies can provide family life education programs that are focused on both children and adults. According to Hughes and Schroeder (1997), such programs for children have several purposes:

to teach children that there are many different types of families

to discuss emotions that accompany changes in families

to discuss communication and problem-solving techniques (pp. 287–288).

Adult-based programs, which are more common, provide a forum to discuss changing family dynamics and ways in which to establish closeness and "a sense of common experience" (p. 289). These programs also deal with issues of transitional adjustment, including emotions of loss and guilt, changing roles and boundaries, and myths about stepfamily life in general.

All families going through structural changes need social support through community-based life education programs, extended family, and friends. Whether a family is single-parented or blended, they may find that societal attitudes can be both a source of help and a source of stress. The boundary between family struc-

> *The boundary between family structure and outside culture is dynamic and reciprocal; each influences the other.*

ture and outside culture is dynamic and reciprocal; each influences the other. As such, the contextual dialectics of public and private, and of real and ideal, are very much in evidence when considering structure. Societal judgments and expectations for family functioning that are based on the nuclear structure, for example, may hinder development within a given blended family. This is true for adults and children who must "confront their own expectations regarding what parents are and what they are supposed to do without embracing models of behavior that will not work in a stepfamily situation" (Hughes & Schroeder, 1997, p. 287). Although part of the problem in embracing diverse family structures is gaining societal approval, at least part of the solution must come through cultural change. The American family is as rich in cultural diversity as it is in structural variety. Furthermore, "The approach to transforming family curriculum by including diverse family experiences must be integrative, not merely additive" (Allen & Farnsworth, 1993, p. 352). This means that the study of stepfamilies must take into account their "structural complexity and diversity" and go beyond an approach in which problems are "studied to the near exclusion of positive interactions" (Coleman, Ganong, & Fine, 2000, p. 1288). Just as we appreciate the richness of diversity in structure, we must embrace cultural diversity among families. In so doing, we expose our assumptions about what we consider real and ideal. Chapter 4 further explores the cultural diversity of American families.

4

Cultural Diversity in the New American Family

The increasingly diverse society in which families live is one that offers great richness as well as great confusion. Trying to maintain a dominant ideology through hegemonic practices, researchers and policymakers sometimes fail to address the diversity. "Images of the 'Normal American Family' are pervasive in the dominant culture" and are part of a public rhetoric "found in the discourse of politicians, social commentators, and moral leaders; in the tasks of everyday interactions; and in movies, television shows, and books" (Pyke, 2000, p. 241). Just as the nuclear structure has been held up as the normative standard, the culture of Euro-American, heterosexual, Christian families is often regarded as the norm (Allen & Farnsworth, 1993). We may ignore outright families that deviate from this cultural norm or regard them as inferior, or even suspect at times that their composition undermines the American family.

Culture influences the way that families experience and construct reality (Pyke, 2000). Even within groups that appear to be culturally and structurally similar, heterogeneity will exist. Our assumptions about nuclear, white, middleclass, Christian families do not accurately predict the behavior of all

> *Our assumptions about nuclear, white, middle-class, Christian families do not accurately predict the behavior of all families who fit these categories.*

families who fit these categories. In fact, although "prevailing family images emphasize sensitivity, open honest communication, flexibility, and forgiveness," these traits may be less important or even contrary in cultures that stress "duty, responsibility, obedience, and a commitment to the family collective that supercedes self-interest" (Pyke, 2000, p. 241).

Beyond the fact that each cultural group experiences within-group change, the culture at large is also dynamic and changing. As an example, if we describe the traditional family from the 1950s compared with the traditional family of the 1990s, our descriptions would not be the same (Coontz, 2000). But because "studies of structural change of families constitute a major portion of family-related literature of the last decade" (McLoyd, Cauce, Takeuchi, & Wilson, 2000, p. 1070), the study of cultural change receives less attention than it has in the past. Furthermore, as Westerhoff (1983) asserts, change in the family is not new. In fact, any given trend we see in the American family, such as fewer children or dual income-earners, can reverse itself rapidly. What becomes important, then, is that, rather than trying to control the direction of change through value-laden prescriptions, we, instead, respond to the needs of families in all their current variations.

To respond adequately, we must first recognize Westerhoff's (1983) "Myth of the Fall":

Once upon a time there was the ideal extended family in which all persons lived harmoniously in an ideal world where everyone had an assigned role and knew what was expected of them; and then the family fell from grace. (p. 251)

Today's families deviate from the norm of the mythical family in culture as well as structure. Whereas Chapter 3 described how structure defines family membership and boundaries, culture illustrates how families live within those boundaries. The diverse cultural backgrounds of family members contribute to the styles that they develop to manage contextual and interactional dialectical forces. For purposes of this chapter, let's define culture as Montgomery (1992b) does: the "laws, rules, customs, stories, suggestions, and directions that guide couples in the conduct of their relationships" (p. 475). As used here, we broaden the definition to include families as well as couples. Although cultures differ in numerous ways, this chapter focuses on three main variables that influence diversity in American family life generally, and their dialectical management specifically. These variables are

- religion
- sexual orientation
- race.

In our efforts to define and understand these variables, we will review exemplary rather than exhaustive literature and examine examples of how these manifest themselves in family life. In real families, cultural variations are not so easy to separate because

> *In real families, cultural variations are not so easy to separate because they evolve and interact together.*

they evolve and interact together, but for the sake of clarity here, we treat them individually.

❖ RELIGION AND FAMILY CULTURE

According to Westerhoff (1983), "The family is a relative config-uration, culturally and historically determined, of which there are countless variants" (p. 253). Structural and cultural patterns, historically, change constantly to meet changing social realities, which are not "either good or evil, but like all other social realities, occasions for both" (p. 253). What Westerhoff and others believe helps these changes work for the good of humanity is when the church is included—as well as political, social, and economic institutions—into the culture of family. In this way, the church can become "a fundamental resource for the humanization of all human life" (Westerhoff, 1983, p. 253). Miller (2000) tends to agree: "Religion is a powerful and pervasive force in shaping families" (p. 173). Although we estimate that 90% of Americans across a variety of religions claim to have a religious affiliation, only 44% attend church regularly. Church attendance alone, therefore, is not an adequate measure of how religion can influence the family.

What the Church Expects of the Christian Family

The church as an institution can mandate restrictive cultural definitions for family life. The church expects the "Christian family," for example, to be structured into a "framework where men and women play particular defined roles" (Westerhoff, 1983, p. 254). However, because family structure and culture are highly variable, "We gain nothing by constructing in our imagi-nations the 'perfect family' or a 'Christian family' in terms of outward characteristics" (p. 254). Although 86% of those who claim to have some religious identification consider themselves to be Christian, three denominations (Roman Catholic, Southern Baptist, and Methodist) make up 50% of the Christian population. Among Christians, then, "Religions differ in the degree to which they emphasize intellectualism, formal belief systems, and religious education as opposed to personal experience and meanings ascribed to events" (Miller, 2000, p. 173).

This means that some religions are more conservative than others. A constrained notion of the Christian family will not accurately reflect what is "healthiest or best" for them. Whether a family is Christian or not "depends upon

> *The church as an institution can mandate restrictive cultural definitions for family life.*

the faith of its members and the character of life it shares and not upon its structure, the roles persons play within it, or even the functions it performs" (Westerhoff, 1983, p. 254).

The Nurturing, Supportive Christian Church

The church can become an institution that actively welcomes and supports diversity rather than a place that condemns it (Nakhaima & Dicks, 1995). Through pastoral care, the crises and transitions that families face, such as divorce, can provide the potential for "a 'spiritual turn' that can result in richer, more accountable, and healthy living with other family members and with God" (Miller, 2000, p. 178). Those individuals and groups whom society and fundamentalist religions have marginalized can, instead, be embraced and nurtured as human beings who are "created in the image of a loving God" (p. 176). We can view the divorced family, the single-parent family, the blended family, and the dual-orientation family with homosexual parents and/or children as providing a "context for love, interpersonal commitment and communion" (p. 176). Furthermore, the church can provide occasions to normalize diversity through such rites as baptism, marriage preparation, and funeral services. The

Bible itself contains examples of diversity that would render "romanticized and idealized notions of family living" (p. 177) meaningless.

The Restrictive, Condemning Christian Church

> *The church can provide occasions to normalize diversity through such rites as baptism, marriage preparation, and funeral services.*

A more restrictive notion of Christian values proposes to diminish, rather than support, diversity. In his treatise on divorce, for example, McManus (1994) proclaims that it is the job of organized religion "to strengthen marriage commitment" (p. 50). He maintains that the "central reason for the dissolution of two-parent families is that couples no longer marry for life" (p. 50). We can use this simplified explanation of a complex issue as a basis for judgment, as McManus has. Rather than accepting divorce rates as a cultural fact, McManus believes that the church should change itself to reverse the trend. As a part of the problem of divorce, McManus declares that the church has become a "blessing machine" and a "wedding factory," wherein it marries 75% of new couples, 60% of which do not remain married for life (p. 51). The solution, he contends, is for organized religion to prepare rigorous premarital instruction that endorses chastity and condemns premarital cohabitation, which he considers to be "a cancer on the family" (p. 51). He bases this endorsement on statistics that compare virgin to nonvirgin divorce rates, with nonvirgins being "71% more likely to divorce than those who are virgins on their wedding night" (p. 51). Although he does not indicate whether these statistics refer to males, females, or both, he does indicate that assault statistics on cohabitating females by their male partners is 60% more likely than for married women, and concludes that "men respect wives—not live-in girlfriends" (p. 51). From this view, organized religion's role in preventing divorce is to provide marital instruction prior to the wedding night that will encourage chastity and improve communication.

Along with McManus, a group of pastors from Baptist churches in California spearheaded a movement called "Community Marriage Policy" whose concern is to "radically reduce the divorce rate among those married in area churches" (p. 56). They attempt to accomplish their

> *A more restrictive notion of Christian values proposes to diminish, rather than support, diversity.*

mission by a mandatory four-month involvement from couples intending to be married in their churches. This premarital programming is oriented around raising the level of commitment between those people who marry in the church. The movement has spread to cities in other states and includes couples' participation in marital inventories, engagement programs, mentoring by older church couples before and after the wedding, and training couples "whose marriages were once rocky to work with troubled couples" (p. 56). Although this programming may indeed enhance the marriages of couples who embrace this version of Christianity, it will not be applicable to everyone.

Do Family Values Equal Christian Values?

According to Heim (1996), we sometimes use "family values" and "Christian values" synonymously, and generally they reference restrictive notions of diversity. A point of criticism regarding a conservative notion of family/Christian values is that it often condemns "those on the social underside" (p. 104). Some critics of family/Christian values maintain that "the white middle class try to preserve their intact families at the expense of the economically and socially deprived whose conditions make it a challenge for their intactness" (p. 105). In other words, the intactness, or commitment, between family members depends not only on the virginal status of the couple at the time of marriage but also on a complex host of factors that interacts with the resultant structure. When Christianity is based on how families live, rather than their structures, economics, or race, we gain a more open view of diversity. Heim continues: "It is ironic that the people who want to preserve family values are often the greatest defenders of capitalism," which supports "commercial involvement in sexuality, exploitation, and pornography" (p. 106). To the extent, then, that the church emphasizes family values "in isolation from economic, procreational, educational, and political dimensions," it will not really be relevant; in fact, its critics contend that "the blaming, judgmental kind of rhetoric around family issues is part of the moral collapse in our culture" (p. 107).

According to Miller (2000), "Religion provides and helps shape values, morality, and family structure, even when family members may not be aware of this influence" (p. 174). As such, scholars need to reconsider the impact of religion in families, the "need to diversify definitions of religious involvement to include more personalized and autonomous spiritual beliefs" that go beyond church attendance (Miller, 2000, p. 174). Miller believes that religion plays a multifaceted role and "provides a sense of community—a sort of 'extended family' that witnesses the milestones and provides support and guidance, especially during times of crisis" (2000, p. 173).

> *When Christianity is based o how families live, rather than their structures, economics, or race, we gain a more open view of diversity.*

Religion's Effect on Dialectical Contradictions

How might religion as a cultural factor in family life affect the management of dialectical contradictions? Through various management strategies, we can deal with the contextual dialectics, which include the private/public and ideal/real dimensions as well as the interactional dialectics of independence/dependence, judgment/acceptance, expression/protection, and affection/instrumentality. As we have discussed in previous chapters, families commonly exhibit patterns of dialectical management that include selection, separation, neutralization, and reformulation. A fundamentalist Christian, for example, may select only the "ideal" polarity of family life and ignore and deny any discrepancies between the ideal (as defined by his or her religious beliefs)

The separation strategy could be used to manage the private/public dialectic by exhibiting Christian behavior temporally; many families may perform the public act of attending church on Sundays but privately depart from Christian ways throughout the week.

and the actual experience. Some parents who take the biblical reference to sparing the rod and spoiling the child to its selective extreme may decide to forego any expression of leniency. The separation strategy could be used to manage the private/public dialectic by exhibiting Christian behavior temporally; many families may perform the public act of attending church on Sundays but privately depart from Christian ways throughout the week. A family might decide to separate the dialectic topically; for example, they may agree with church doctrine on the issue of abortion but disagree with doctrine about women's role in marriage.

The Christian family who uses neutralization to manage the dialectical tension between the ideal and real may conceive that even the most ideal families fall short of perfection and thus, they may accept their own shortcomings as evidence of their human nature as practicing religious persons. A family could reformulate the tension by deciding that the more real a family is, the more ideal it becomes, thus transcending the contradiction. Given a specific religious orientation, certain patterns will be more or less likely to emerge. Although here we have described only conservative and nonconservative Christianity, the religious leanings of American families remain vast and will variously influence family culture and dialectical management.

❖ DIVERSITY IN SEXUAL ORIENTATION

Perhaps no topic provokes so explosive a discussion as the topic of same-sex marriage. Just as interracial marriage was once considered abhorrent and was illegal in many states, marriage and adoption rights for gay men and lesbians are today's new frontier for the family. In their attempt to achieve the legal rights that are automatically given to male and female couples who wish to marry and raise children, gay- and lesbian-headed households are "changing the definition of family from one based on law to one based on emotional bonds and family ties" (Allen & Wilcox, 2000, p. 57). Many Americans, through either religious or private belief systems, exhibit heterosexism or prejudice against sexual orientations that are not exclusively heterosexual. Whereas discrimination based on age, race, religion, national origin, and gender is illegal, most states grant homosexuals very few basic human rights, whether in the family, the community, or the workplace.

Although in the past, homosexuality was associated with mostly negative attributions, lesbian and gay family members continue to be denied basic human rights, such as the right to marry and raise children. We estimate that 1.5 million lesbians are mothers and a half million gay men are fathers (West &

Turner, 2000, p. 147), but, because of their sexual orientation, society denies these people the legal rights associated with parenting. As once happened with inter-racial couples, often times gay men and lesbians are victims of hate crimes, including murder.

> *Just as interracial marriage was once considered abhorrent and was illegal in many states, marriage and adoption rights for gay men and lesbians are today's new frontier for the family.*

In this section, we consider sexual orientation a factor of diversity. As Allen and Wilcox (2000) ask, "How would the world be different if gay, lesbian, and bisexual families had the same rights and privileges as heterosexual families?" (p. 60). Just as families adopt different religions and have various ethnic and racial identities, they also exhibit variations in sexual orienta-tions. Not all people are heterosexual, which means that many families are made up of parents or children or both who are homosexual. Because homophobia, or the irrational fear of homosexuals, may prevent society at large from recognizing the gifted nature and enormous contributions of people who make known their homosexuality, many of these people choose to remain closeted. When the legal right to marry, to adopt or bear children, to receive health benefits afforded to spouses or part-ners, and to be protected from hate crimes are at stake, the pri-vate nature of homosexuality in the family becomes a more public matter.

Dual-Orientation Families

We often describe families with a member or members who have diverse sexual orientations as "gay" or "lesbian families," but we might more accurately describe them as *dual-orientation families* (Murphy, 1998). Among men and women who are in

> *Because homophobia, or the irrational fear of homosexuals, may prevent society at large from recognizing the gifted nature and enormous contributions of people who make known their homosexuality, many of these people choose to remain closeted.*

same-sex relationships, 45% to 80% of lesbians and 40% to 60% of gay men consider themselves to be in committed relationships (Allen & Wilcox, 2000). Just as we consider families with a male and female parent who work outside of the home to be dual-career families, the family with a homosexual member is dual-oriented; in other words, not every family member is lesbian or gay.

Myths About Dual-Orientation Families

Many myths surround dual-oriented families, most of them based on ignorance and, therefore, on fear of the unknown. For example, gay or lesbian parents are not more likely to raise gay or lesbian children; sexual orientation is not something that can be taught in the family. Studies show that children who are raised in same-sex households do not differ in their gender identity, role behavior, and sexual orientation from children raised in households headed by heterosexual parents (Patterson, 2000). Further, Allen and Wilcox (2000) report finding that children raised in dual-orientation households gain some advantages over children raised in heterosexual families:

- experiencing a multicultural environment
- observing androgynous role behavior
- belonging to an intentional family in which relationships are based "not only on biological or genetic relationships but also on love, self-definition, and choice" (p. 57)
- forging strong ties to the gay community.

These advantages suggest that dialectical management in dual-oriented families may reflect more adaptability than in other family cultures.

In addition to myths about gay and lesbian parenting, the myth exists that same-sex couples mimic heterosexual marriage roles, with one partner acting as the wife and the other as the husband. In reality,

> *Studies show that children who are raised in same-sex households do not differ in their gender identity, role behavior, and sexual orientation from children raised in households headed by heterosexual parents.*

what happens to these roles when two women, for example, choose to form an intentional family? Because the couple may have few same-sex role models from which to draw, patterns of behavior and responsibility tend to emerge over time rather than to be predetermined. The women must negotiate and develop role patterns that fit their individual skills, abilities, and interests. Although the quality of their relationships may be equivalent to that of heterosexual married couples, gay and lesbian couples exhibit more autonomy and equality, although less longevity, than do heterosexual couples (Allen & Wilcox, 2000). Murphy (1998) describes homosexual relational patterns as stressing "role flexibility, equality, and shared decision-making" (p. 350).

Because it is currently impossible for gay and lesbian couples to confirm their commitment through marriage legally recognized by any of the 50 states,[1] dual-orientation families tend to work out their patterns in private. Without the benefit of the social validation we grant to heterosexual couples, viable relationships of same-sex couples are vulnerable. As same-sex couples validate their own culture outside of the values that society places on relationships, implications for the dialectic of stability and change emerge. In other words, without societal support, same-sex couples may be more vulnerable and, at the same time, more driven to succeed in their relationships.

The Reality of Dual-Oriented Families

> *As same-sex couples validate their own culture outside of the values that society places on relationships, implications for the dialectic of stability and change emerge.*

Research on dual-oriented families provides a much different and more positive view of their experienced realities. Like any other group drawn together by a commonality, dual-oriented families are not all alike. Instead, they exhibit within-group differences. They are diverse in their religious backgrounds, ethnicity, race, education, politics, and income. Structurally, dual-oriented families may be single-parent or represented by couples who have children together, but Allen and Wilcox (2000) found that "because gay fathers and lesbian mothers often become parents in the context of hetero-sexual marriage, blended families are probably the most common type" (p. 56).

According to Laird (1996), "Lesbian and gay male families come in many shapes and sizes" (p. 559). Sometimes, a lesbian or gay partner has been previously married and brings children from that marriage into the new, same-sex partnership. A couple may be exclusively homosexual but, through adoption or artificial insemination of one of the partners, may become parents of children they call their own. Although these children are not more likely to grow up gay, they have more cross-gender contact and face more social discrimination than children in families headed by heterosexuals. As a result of society's heterosexism and homophobia, these children may be "handicapped by the secrecy and invisibility that characterize gay family life" (p. 564). This means that a dialectic tension of public and private may take on special meanings in dual-oriented families. Regardless of the challenges they may encounter, dual-oriented families lead everyday lives with both strengths and the potential for dysfunction, just as we find with other families. In this sense, then, dual-oriented families are no more disadvantaged than other families.

In addition to dealing with same-sex marriage, some parents must confront the issue of their own child's homosexuality. Whether they themselves are heterosexual or homosexual, when parents assume that their children are heterosexual, they

> *Regardless of the challenges they may encounter, dual-oriented families lead everyday lives with both strengths and the potential for dysfunction, just as we find with other families. In this sense, then, dual-oriented families are no more disadvantaged than other families.*

will be surprised to discover that one, or more, of them is lesbian or gay. Research on the discovery process reveals that family dynamics prior to coming out are related to "post-discovery experiences" (Ben-Ari, 1995, p. 89). Although few systematic studies are available, there is some evidence that the coming-out process unfolds in three stages: prediscovery, discovery, and postdiscovery. Although the entire process reflects family tendencies toward disclosure and avoidance, each stage also contains its own thematic content. As an example, the prediscovery stage is characterized by the dialectical tension of simultaneously wanting to come out and fearing to come out. In his study of the coming-out process of 32 gay men and women in the San Francisco area, Ben-Ari (1995) found that nearly two-thirds were fearful during this stage. Interacting with this fear was the extent to which these children "perceived their parents to have past experience, direct or indirect, of homosexuality" (p. 97). Also, the public/private dialectic, so pertinent during the coming-out stage, involves managing the fear of being rejected while being motivated by "a need not to hide or live a lie" (Allen & Wilcox, 2000, p. 54).

During the act of discovery, Ben-Ari (1995) found that "how parents learned about their child's sexual preference, the modes of disclosure, and the information that was disclosed were the three most important topics" (p. 97). The majority of the participants in his study came out to one parent, initially their mothers, in face-to-face settings, using direct statements such as, "I am gay" (pp. 100–101). Following the discovery act, subjects reported a variety of parental reactions ranging from shock and anger to acknowledgment and acceptance. Over time, the more negative reactions subsided and acceptance increased.

This research provides an example of how the awareness of sexual orientation diversity and integration into the family's identity is a process occurring over time. In one study, the process of older parents coming to terms with having a gay child involved several transitions: (a) moving away from denial to advocacy, (b) mobilizing in love, and (c) facing their own unresolved issues (Allen & Wilcox, 2000). Patterson (2000) found that a two-stage process occurred when the homosexual orientation of a family member became known. First, "family members struggle to understand and assimilate this new information about one of its members" (p. 1064). Accordingly, they either reject the information or reorganize to accommodate the shift in identity. For all family members, the process takes time. We have only begun to study the dialectical management of the change surrounding the acceptance of a family member's homosexuality, but this research will be critical to our understanding of family dialectics.

Same-Sex Adult Relationships

Just as children coming out to their parents is a process, so is the formation of same-sex adult relationships. A discussion of same-sex relationship development "is necessarily embedded within a larger context of belief systems about gender and sexual orientation" (Murphy, 1998, p. 345). Allen and Wilcox (2002) believe that "the most important factor for determining the psychological well-being for older lesbians is the level of homophobia in society and in oneself" (p. 58). Our culture tends to treat gender as dichotomous, labeling its enactment as either normal (men as masculine and women as feminine) or pathological (everyone else). Thus "attempts to normalize their experiences result in many gay and lesbian people saying 'we are just like you' to the straight community" (Murphy, 1998, p. 345). Because both partners are of the same biological sex, they face adversity in the larger social context; as a result, they must also "grieve the loss of heterosexual privilege" (p. 347). What privilege? One example is that not all heterosexuals choose to marry, but all have the legal right to marry. Not so, partners of same-sex relationships. If the partners themselves are at different stages of grieving this loss of privilege, "they may feel surprise and anger at the other's sadness" (p. 348).

Stage differences in the coming-out process affect relational development patterns. The partners' decision to disclose or conceal their sexual orientations from their families

> *Our culture tends to treat gender as dichotomous, labeling its enactment as either normal (men as masculine and women as feminine) or pathological (everyone else).*

and in their workplaces also has consequences for their dialectical management. Same-sex couples may choose to separate their public and private lives by concealing their relationships publicly, or enacting them as nonintimate, while reserving expressions of coupleness for private settings, either alone or among similarly oriented friends. When both partners conceal their identity to others, they may fail to develop a support network and become isolated, which separates them from the culture. If others repeatedly invalidate their disclosure, they can experience distance regulation problems, such as fusion, or a state of enmeshment. The management of the autonomy/connection dialectic, via separation, results in isolation from community and fusion in relationship with each other.

Another separation strategy for managing the tension of autonomy/connection might be to topically maintain autonomy in the workplace (i.e., concealing orientation) but to be connected in the extended family (i.e., coming out to parents and siblings). Same-sex couples may negotiate neutralized patterns by which they let others know through verbal revelations that they are intimately related, but they do not act out their intimacy physically (e.g., by holding hands or kissing) in the presence of others. The reformulation strategy could be used to reframe their dialectical autonomy and connection. They may, for example, contend that the autonomy they gain as a result of concealing their homosexual orientation enables them to be truly connected. In these ways, management of their dialectical tensions can contribute to and influence the differential pattern of relational development that emerges for same-sex couples. Because of the cultural constraints imposed on dual-orientation families, they will experience their own unique dialectical challenges.

❖ RACIAL AND ETHNIC DIVERSITY

The current census conducted by the United States government contained more categories for the identification of race/ethnicity than did any previous census. In recognition of the diverse ethnicity and color of people who live in this country, the government presented a number of hyphenated options, including African-American, Asian-American, Chinese-American, Euro-American, Japanese-American, and Latin-American, as well as a category for "other." According to McLoyd, Cauce, Takeuchi, and Wilson

(2000), "In the 21st Century, our country will no longer be overwhelmingly White. . . . It will instead be fully multicultural, equally divided between non-Hispanic European Americans and those of other racial and ethnic groups" (p. 1070). They predict further that by the year 2050, "Our nation will consist of a population that is 8% Asian-American, 14% African-American, 25% Hispanic, and 53% non-Hispanic White" (p. 1070). Contributing to the cultural diversity of family life in the United States are the attendant rules, roles, norms, customs, and so forth that differentiate racial heritages. These elements of culture are a resource for family members as they relate to each other (interactional dialectics) and as they relate to society at large (contextual dialectics). As the racial and ethnic cultures of American families continue to diversify, we need to recognize the variables that affect their dialectical management and, ultimately, the quality of their experiences. We must work to replace our stereotyped images of families with accurate and timely portrayals. Why, for example, do stereotypes of patriarchal Latino families persist "despite the fact that 44% are female-headed" (McLoyd, Cauce, Takeuchi, & Wilson, 2000, p. 1075)?

The Blending of the American Family

As people of diverse racial and ethnic backgrounds have intermarried, the American family has taken on numerous cultural blends. As of 1995, 246,000 of 50 million marriages were between African-Americans and Euro-Americans. Marriages

> *In recognition of the diverse ethnicity and color of people who live in this country, the government presented a number of hyphenated options, including African-American, Asian-American, Chinese-American, Euro-American, Japanese-American, and Latin-American, as well as a category for "other."*

between people of Hispanic and non-Hispanic heritage have doubled to more than 1 million since 1970. Furthermore, 60% of Japanese-American children in the United States have one white parent, and 40% of Asian/Pacific Islanders co-parent with a white partner. Native American children are more likely to have one white parent than two Indian parents. Current shifts in immigration patterns, with a change from 80% Euro-American in 1960 to 80% Latino, Caribbean, and Asian in the 1990s, make it likely that intercultural families will continue to increase.

Conflicting Cultural Values in Couples

Multiethnic families often face oppression as they attempt to meet the demands of conflicting cultural values (Graham, Moeai, & Shizuru, 1985). In studies of interethnic couples, researchers identified a number of differences associated with the culture of the family-of-origin, including variations in: customs (such as gift-giving), languages, styles of conflict resolution, and attitudes toward child-rearing. Furthermore, in their methods of adjusting to these conflicting values, multiethnic couples displayed a range of dialectical management strategies. Some couples used selection strategies by which one of the spouses completely adopted the other's cultural values, foregoing their own. In addition to selection, some couples used temporal separation, by which they adhered sometimes to one partner's customs and sometimes to the other's. Some couples neutralized their ethnic and racial heritages by agreeing to a solution that was somewhere in between their family of origin's positions; others reformulated and created their own, brand-new style.

Conflicting Cultural Values in Families:
The Example of Elian Gonzalez

Families also experience intracultural diversity, by which divergences within their cultures can generate conflict. The management of dialectical tensions in an intracultural family was made apparent in the case of Elian Gonzalez, the six-year-old Cuban refugee who was rescued in 1999 off the Miami, Florida, coast. After Elian survived the death of his fellow travelers, including his mother, his Cuban-American relatives attempted to get permission for

> *Multiethnic families often face oppression as they attempt to meet the demands of conflicting cultural values.*

him to emigrate from Cuba to the United States. The custody fight between Elian's Miami relatives, who have been immigrating to the U.S. since 1965, and his family members who remain in Cuba, including his biological father, was a landmark case in intra- and intercultural tradition and law.

The Gonzalez family is headed by Luis and Georgina, who remain in Cuba; their nine children, including Elian's grandfather Juan Gonzalez, have divided themselves between Miami and Cuba—six of the children immigrated to the United States, while three (including Elian's grandfather Juan) remain in Cuba. Their children, of which Elian's father Juan Miguel is one, also remain divided between their loyalties to their Cuban heritage and their desire to live in Miami. Of Elian's nine aunts and uncles, seven have immigrated to the United States, while two of them, plus his own father, remain in Cuba. This complex history, which was brought into public awareness due to unusual circumstances, sheds light on the custody battle that was fought between Elian's Miami relatives, who wanted to save him from what they saw as an oppressive Cuban upbringing, and his own father, who believed in the legacy of his Cuban heritage. Thus, the issues they fought over were based on the diverse cultural values between Cuban-Americans and Cubans (Golden, 2000).

Other Families, Other Conflicting Values

Just as researchers incorrectly assume the structure of real families to be nuclear, some researchers have incorrectly assumed that real families are white. We are now increasingly aware that real families come in many colors.

Asian-Americans represent a significant ethnic group within the United States. "Given the relatively high percentage of Asian-American families that are extended, researchers who focus exclusively on parents and children as the operational measure of the family unit are prone to lose sight of the social and cultural resources that other relatives bring to Asian-American families" (McLoyd, Cauce, Takeuchi, & Wilson, 2000, p. 1072). The same authors note that there is a "lack of empirical study on marital relations among Asian-Americans" (p. 1074). Instead, researchers tend to rely on outdated or Eurocentric notions to evaluate these couples.

Another racial group that represents the cultural diversity of the family in America is African Americans. Many would argue that African Americans have faced more cultural oppression than any other racial group. With a history of forced immigration through slavery, the roots of African American families are ancient and tangled. When forced to merge two diverse cultures—life in one's own native country and a life of slavery in a foreign culture—patterns of survival will emerge. Although slavery is no longer legally practiced, these patterns persist as white and black Americans gradually change their perceptions of each other. All families could benefit through an appreciation of the unique qualities that come from an African-American cultural heritage. For example, with the advent of dual-career families, many white parents have a better appreciation of the African American tradition of using their extended family for child-rearing.

As we do with other ethnic groups, we assume that African Americans are homogeneous, that is, similar in attitudes, beliefs, values, and backgrounds. This assumption has been the breeding ground for skewed images of African American families that do not accurately reflect their diverse within-group experiences. For instance, we often construe the African American family as being single-parent with a mother or grandmother at the head, living on welfare, living in a dangerous inner-city environment, and raising children that will be involved with crime (i.e., drugs and violence) and, if male, will eventually be imprisoned. Few studies on families of color use longitudinal or observational methods, however. Furthermore, although "core knowledge on family processes among Euro-Americans is based on normative studies . . . that on people of color is based on follow-ups of high-risk families" that poses a "grave danger that our work will reinforce common stereotypes and prejudices" (McLoyd, Cauce, Takeuchi, & Wilson, 2000, p. 1087). Although such a description may accurately describe some African American families' circumstances, it overlooks the reality that most of these families experience.

According to Thompson (1998), the African American family has been characterized as inherently deficient. Through a number of studies of African American families, however, it is apparent that they exhibit great resiliency in the face of challenge. As Thompson explains, "The elements of adaptation, culture, and choice are important in understanding how Blacks resist oppression. Foremost has been the development of a kinship system that has persisted even against great adversity" (p. 50). Thus, rather than concentrating on deficits, it is more constructive to identify the resources that African American families have mobilized to face their own particular stresses in American society. These include supportive social networks, flexible relationships within the family, strong religious affiliations, interdependence with extended family, adoption of fictive kin (who are, for example, nonblood relations who are called "aunt" or "uncle") and strong identification with their racial group (McAdoo, 1998). This list of resources demonstrates how family definitions can be based on a number of criteria that reflect not only physical relationships but functional and interactional relationships as well.

A major function of all families is the socialization of their children. Although "parents of color and white parents alike talk to their children about race . . . they do so with very different goals. Whereas white parents discuss race with children to promote attitudes of tolerance and equality, African-American parents' discussions of race with their children tend to focus on preparing their children for prejudice" (McLoyd, Cauce, Takeuchi, & Wilson, 2000, p. 1085). In the African American family, children face the unique challenge of having to simultaneously learn the system that oppresses them and also learn how to resist and change it (Thompson, 1998). Thus, the dialectical contradictions faced in the socialization of black children stem from three sources of influence.

Mainstream culture. First, black children are influenced by the mainstream culture, with its idolization of white, middle-class families. Sometimes black family members are criticized if they are too heavily influenced by the white, mainstream culture. In a fascinating book, *Our Kind of People: Inside America's Black Upper Class*, the author, L. O. Graham (2000), refers to the wholesale adoption of mainstream culture by some black people as "passing" for white. As an extreme, passing occurs when a black person rejects his or her racial identity and exclusively takes on the culture of mainstream, white America. Whereas the black elite consider passing taboo, non-elite blacks consider elite blacks, as a group, to be trying to pass. In his study of the black upper class, Graham identifies numerous similarities between the traditions of the black upper class and the traditions of the white upper class (e.g., exclusivity in club memberships). A member of an elite black family himself, Graham describes his experience as similar to those in an affluent white culture, including attendance at exclusive boarding schools, camps, and colleges, and membership in exclusive social clubs.

Minority experience. In addition to the mainstream influence on socialization, African American children are also influenced by their experience as a minority group in a mainstream white culture. The socialization of African American children is affected by the social, economic, and political conditions in which they exist. Although this minority experience will not be universal—within-group conditions may be vastly different—outsiders hold the minority position constant by tending not to recognize the group's heterogeneity.

Unique cultural experience. The third influence on black children's socialization is their unique cultural experience, including "styles, motifs, and patterns of behavior that are unique to blacks" (Thompson, 1998, p. 57).

The contextual dialectics that face black families, therefore, will reflect their mainstream, minority, and cultural experiences. In dealing with the contextual contradictions of culture—the public/private dialectic, for example—through selection, African American family members may choose to pass as white, totally hiding their heritage from the public. Privately, other family members would know of their black identity. A family may use topical separation when they practice the rule of "Don't talk about blacks in front of whites," maintaining public solidarity but allowing for private dissension. Some families neutralize the contextual dialectic of the ideal/real. In *Our Kind of People*, Graham (2000) discusses how many elite black families had their children participate in Jack and Jill, an exclusive preparatory organization for the socialization of African American children into the upper class, as well as attend private schools that were racially integrated. The family that opts for reformulation of the ideal/real dialectic may reframe race as a matter of humanity instead of color; thus, black, white, and all other racial groups would be considered as one race—the human race.

Sometimes family members dialectically manage the interface between culture and family consciously but without awareness. In other words, it is unlikely that a family of any racial or ethnic background would sit down and say, "Okay, now it's time to negotiate our dialectical tensions. Let's start with the contextual dialectic of the ideal and real." Each family's choices in dialectical

> *Each family's choices in dialectical management may, however, have far-reaching consequences for the quality of family life that they experience.*

management may, however, have far-reaching consequences for the quality of family life that they experience. Throughout this chapter and in Chapter 3, we have focused on diversity, both cultural and structural. For the sake of discussion, we have treated each source of diversity separately. In the next chapter, we will examine the interaction of culture and structure in our approaches to, and patterns of, family development.

❖ NOTE

1. As of this writing, Vermont offers civil union status to gay and lesbian couples, and in California, same-sex couples who register their status with the secretary of state are granted many of the rights previously reserved for married heterosexual couples.

5

Developmental Diversity

In addition to their cultures and structures, families vary in their developmental patterns and individual family members. Relationships between family members grow and change over time. The manner in which families manage the dialectical tensions of stability and change, as well as autonomy and connection, and the ways families combine culture and structure can result in numerous developmental patterns. In this chapter, we review several approaches to family development and discuss specific models that illustrate change patterns in blended and dual-orientation families.

❖ APPROACHES TO DEVELOPMENT

Regardless of their particular structures and cultures, all families change over time. The families of five, ten, or twenty years ago will exhibit some major shifts and probably many minor changes in relational patterns. Although families are actually works in progress, we often think of them as static entities. Our conceptions can hamper acceptance of change in the family at both the societal and the personal levels. When we view our family as static, it may take on a nostalgic characteristic and, instead of changing and moving forward, our family may strive to preserve a romanticized version of what it once was.

> *When we view our family as static, it may take on a nostalgic characteristic and, instead of changing and moving forward, our family may strive to preserve a romanticized version of what it once was.*

In her book, *Gift from the Sea* (1955), Anne Morrow Lindbergh uses the metaphor of the seashell to describe different stages of family life. Once the family outgrows a given shell, it must move on to its next shell—the family cannot go back to what it once was. We cannot repeat relational states, whether the state is blissful, such as falling in love, or whether it is stressful, as in raising children. A family cannot move backwards to recapture its prior family experience. Instead, each new experience transforms the family so that what it once was, as a family, no longer exists.

The Family Life Cycle Approach

When we characterize a family as homeostatic, favoring stability over change, we see the family's development as a linear, uniform process. The term *family life cycle* describes a sequence of developmental phases through the passage of time wherein members of the nuclear family enter, grow, and exit. Each stage requires the performance of important life tasks in order to grow into the next stage. This approach to development assumes a so-called normal progression through family life, with the family's adoption of mainstream ideas about structure and culture.

The life cycle approach is based on predictable change, that is, change that a family living by mainstream cultural values and practices can expect to experience. It is change that is grounded in limited cultural norms and the biological growth of adults and children. This kind of change emphasizes stability, positing that family life consists of mostly stable periods with brief interludes of change in between, known as transitions. We tend to consider a family successful when it lives by culture-conforming values and exhibits a fixed series of developmental stages. If a family deviates from what we prescribe as the norm and does not complete the stages we consider normal, we tend to judge it a failure. Sometimes we even use that term, such as when we describe divorce as a "failed marriage."

> *If a family deviates from what we prescribe as the norm and does not complete the stages we consider normal, we tend to judge it a failure. Sometimes we even use that term, such as when we describe divorce as a "failed marriage."*

What do we consider a normal life-cycle model?

Courtship

Early marriage

Early parenthood

Middle parenthood

Launching

Retirement

Death.

We complete each stage before going on to the next.

Courtship

Courtship, which we assume occurs between a male and a female who are not previously married, involves the process of forming a commitment to marry. Because of the courting couple's determination to form a relationship, we expect the couple to incrementally reveal information about themselves to each other so that they escalate their intimacy in a rational way. By working through their problems and disclosing information in a progressive fashion, courting couples can determine whether the other person is "marriageable." We thus see courtship as a decision-making process used to predict the future (Yerby, Buerkel-Rothfuss, and Bochner, 1995). If the relationship partners make the decision to marry, they will have a brief transition, marked by engagement and wedding plans, before they enter the next stage.

Early Marriage

During the early marriage phase, couples must concentrate on the completion of five tasks that enable them to construct their own marital reality. According to Yerby, Buerkel-Rothfuss, and Bochner (1995), couples must

1. integrate their expectations about marital life

2. co-define reality

3. negotiate a communication code

4. organize their relationship

5. manage their contradictory needs for integration and differentiation

Integrating expectations. To integrate their expectations, which come both from their own experiences and through the culture at large, couples create their own definitions of their marital roles. Some couples release prior expectations and adapt to reality more readily than others, who may be more or less in agreement with the other partner's expectations. When expectations conflict—for example, if one partner has notions of marital roles based on gender and the other person has role expectations based on interests and abilities—the couple may find it more difficult to negotiate the integration of expectations with reality.

Co-defining reality. Another task of early marriage involves the co-defining of reality. When newly married couples co-define reality, they reconstruct their perceptions, identities, and beliefs from the past through their current relationship. Perceptions about prior relationships, especially those with unmarried friends, are altered. In many cases, newly married couples find themselves developing new friendships with other married couples. As they co-define reality, couples will also experience the narrowing of their alternatives. For example, career options that were viable prior to marriage, such as accepting an out-of-state job offer, may become unacceptable.

Negotiating a communication code. As they develop their own preferred styles of relating to each other, couples negotiate communication codes. They decide how they relate in private and public. They may, for example, express affection through terms of endearment in private but be more reserved in public. Couples negotiate their styles of conflict resolution. Based on prior experience in their families of origin, as well as in previous romantic relationships, they may have strong reactions to either aggressive or passive approaches to conflict. As they develop a style that suits both their needs, they must take into account the emotional baggage that often accompanies conflict. Couples negotiate styles of humor, allowing or disallowing behaviors such as sarcasm and teasing as their preferred styles of relating. They will negotiate how they make decisions. They may opt to make joint decisions on major issues but remain autonomous in others. Often, decisions about spending and saving money can become a testing ground for determining an effective style of problem solving.

Organizing the relationship. Couples undertake a process of establishing patterns of control in their relationships. According to a relational view of communication, all messages contain both content and relational information; the *content* is the substance and the *relational information* controls the direction. Sometimes subtly and sometimes blatantly, couples work out the power dimension of their relationships by exhibiting patterns that reflect symmetry and/or complementarity. In a symmetrical pattern, each partner matches the other's behavior, so that if one attempts to dominate, the other will reciprocate in kind. Complementarity patterns occur when partners exhibit directionally opposite behavior—when one attempts to control, the other submits.

Managing integration and differentiation. The final task of early marriage, from this life cycle approach, concerns the management of separateness and togetherness. The dialectical tension of autonomy and connection is central to the couple's early marriage experience. Whereas both partners must pursue their own identity through separateness, they must also develop their relational bond through togetherness. But as Yerby, Buerkel-Rothfuss, and Bochner (1995) point out, "The conditions necessary for the development of identity are likely to be perceived as undermining the couple's stability" (p. 140). Conversely, the conditions that are necessary to establish cohesion may seem to undermine the partners' individual identities. The management strategies for dealing with this dialectic will have important implications for the couple's relational quality.

Early Parenthood

As couples accomplish the tasks of early marriage, the family life cycle model assumes that they will want to have children. Further, the model assumes a couple will decide to have a child, the woman will conceive, and a child will be born. Although many couples have problems with fertility and may have to choose another path to parenting, the life cycle view does not take into account this—or any other—deviation from the plan.

Providing that a couple does conceive and give birth, the addition of an infant to the family will shift the couple's focus from a dyadic relationship to one that is triadic. The marriage partners, now familiar with their husband/wife roles, must learn how to be mothers and fathers. Again, expectations will rise to the surface as the couple negotiates their role responsibilities as parents. Until the 1970s, mothers typically stayed at home and raised their children, while fathers went to work outside the home and earned an income to provide for the family. Now that the majority of families are dual-career, with both parents working outside of the home and both earning income, roles based on gender have blurred. Parenting responsibilities are no longer clear-cut; the more they must be negotiated, the more potential they create for conflict. Thus, this stage of family life tends to be a stressful one.

Middle Parenthood

As children grow through infancy, toddlerhood, early school years, and adolescence, parents will be challenged by their changing needs. Just as early parenthood presents stressful situations, middle parenthood, with the addition of other children complicating the family's development, may also be stressful.

Launching

In the family life cycle model, adolescents will finish high school and then launch into the world of college, military, marriage, or career. At this point, the couple must adjust to a family life that again revolves around them as a couple rather than around parenting their children. During what we sometimes call the "empty nest" time of life, couples may experience relational adjustments as they try to fill the vacancy left in the wake of their prior parental responsibilities. At this stage, grandparenting is often used to fill the gap.

Retirement

According to the family life cycle model, once a couple's children launch themselves into the world, the couple moves toward the latter stages of marriage, beginning with retirement from the occupations one or both partners have held. If their work has determined their identities, retirement can bring a sense of loss that requires adaptation. Retirement also means that couples alter their daily routines and most likely increase their times of togetherness. They must find a way to adjust to these changes at the same time they may feel a loss of their own identities.

Death

The end of the family life cycle model is death; at this point, the family must adapt to the loss of one of its parents or spouses, which affects the family network. If the departed person played a central role in maintaining contact between family members, another member may step up and take on this role.

The family life cycle approach provides a description of what some families may experience as they develop over time; it does not, however, take into account how families develop when they are structurally and culturally diverse. It emphasizes predictable change, with couples staying married and children being conceived and growing in normative ways. It ignores the potential for unpredictable change that families may experience as they face crises and nonnormative events along their way.

A Learning Approach

Somewhat less rigid than the family life cycle view, the learning approach emphasizes qualitative change, or change that results from the unique approaches that families use to adapt over time and through both predictable and unpredictable experiences. The learning approach takes into account that some change will be sequential, with each stage dependent on completion of the previous stage, although not necessarily uniform across families. The learning approach incorporates the diversity that is evident in differing structures and cultures and accounts for this diversity's potential to affect the family's direction of change.

Rather than assuming a normative path to development, the learning approach allows for multiple pathways, dependent on the family's unique structural and cultural features. The diverse pathways that families can exhibit in their developmental process are seen, in part, as a product of their preparedness and skill for moving on to a new stage. The life cycle view, conversely, does not take such variation into account, assuming instead that families will move through the stages whether they are ready or not.

Wynne's (1984) model of development is one example of a learning approach. Through the process of relating to each other over time, families develop across these five learned stages:

1. attachment

2. communicating

3. joint problem solving

4. mutuality

5. intimacy

Thus, the impetus for development comes through interactions, rather than through biological change, as in the life cycle model. Movement between these relational stages builds on prior changes and is based on the development of skills associated with each stage. For example, in the attachment stage, bonds are formed in which family members create a desire to be close to each other during times of distress. During the communicating stage, family members develop shared meanings and are able to take each other's points of view as they de-center from their own personal perspective. In joint problem solving, they learn to manage differences and conflicts. Through mutuality, family members develop their abilities to monitor their progress and redirect when necessary, creating new forms of relating. The intimacy stage involves family members developing the potential for high degrees of emotional sharing and relational risk taking.

The learning approach allows for an understanding of family problems as well as their progress. Because it emphasizes relational development as the basis for family growth, it can be used to examine a family's handling of crisis as well as times of stability. Although the learning approach

> *Through mutuality, family members develop their abilities to monitor their progress and redirect when necessary, creating new forms of relating.*

goes further than the life cycle approach, it still does not go far enough to explain development as contingent on the management of dialectical tensions.

A Dialectical Approach

Stability and change as competing forces are central to a dialectical view of family growth. Whereas the life cycle approach sees change as a momentary episode between long periods of stability, the dialectical approach sees change as the constant, with stability as more momentary. Accordingly, Baxter and Montgomery (1996) propose a rethinking of relationship development. They state, "We take issue with the term 'development' and its underlying ABCDE logic, which is steeped in monologic assumptions of 'progress'" (p. 51). They prefer to use "relationship process" or "relationship change" to describe "movement of a relationship in the course of time" (p. 51). Furthermore, they consider the management of contradiction as the fuel for change, whereas the life cycle approach considers it to be biology, and the learning approach considers it to be skill acquisition. In the dialectical view, a family's patterns manifest themselves as both/and rather than either/or, meaning that families become more and less stable, more and less open, and more and less uncertain as they respond to the "knot of contradictions present at a given point in time" (p. 58). Instead of linear progress, Baxter and Montgomery (1996) use the construct of "dialogic complexity" as a way to capture this *both/and* quality of change.

The notion of dialogic complexity shows how relationship change is emergent and deterministic. Because Baxter and Montgomery consider contradiction "the fundamental 'driver' of change (and stabil-ity) in relationships," they believe their perspective to be loosely deterministic. To the extent that "inner echoes" of socialization experi-ences and "culture's

> *Whereas the life cycle approach sees change as a momentary episode between long periods of stability, the dialectical approach sees change as the constant, with stability as more momentary.*

worldview of what opposes what and which oppositions are 'natural' in personal relationships" are brought to relationships, they are somewhat deterministic (p. 59). However, "over the course of their relationship's history, communicative choices made at Time-1 by the parties are reflected in the choices that seem available to them at Time-2, and so on" (p. 59). To this extent, "a relationship's contradictions" are emergent "in the communicative choices of the moment, but those choices reflect, in part, the constraints of socialization and what transpired in the prior history of the relationship" (p. 59). Relational change, then, can be compared to a discursive chain in which "each link adds something new to the chain but is inherently tied to prior and subsequent links" (p. 59).

We can apply a dialectical approach to family life, which stresses "process" rather than "development," to families of all structural and cultural backgrounds. Consider family process in both structurally and culturally diverse families. Specifically, consider the blended family and how its unique history can influence its developmental process through praxical improvisation. A model of same-sex relationship development highlights the cultural experiences of homosexuals who form a marital union.

The blended family, more common in society than the nuclear family, develops in ways that defy the life cycle model of change. As you will recall, the life cycle model is based on a nuclear bias that can dominate expectations for the stepfamily (Gamache, 1997). However, to the extent that the blended family departs from the path predicted by the life cycle model, it may feel itself to be, or be perceived as being, deficient. Furthermore, "continued use of the 'nuclear family map' masks unique characteristics of the stepfamily" (pp. 41–42). According to Crocker-Lakness (1996), "The stepfamily is formed usually only after some traumatic event such as divorce or the death of a spouse" (p. 1). Unlike nuclear families, "stepfamilies begin already in process, and this places great strains on family relationships" (p. 1). Prior to their loss, they experienced nuclear and/or single-parent life, and they bring this history with them. Accordingly, "The biological parent and children have already established norms, patterns, and relationships which must be reconsidered and redefined" (p. 1).

According to Crosbie-Burnett & McClintic (2000) there are a number of unique transitions that stepfamilies experience, partly due to the fact that they may live in one household or several households "linked together biologically, emotionally, financially, and perhaps legally by children in common" (p. 37). Transitions that Crosbie-Burnett and McClintic document include Initial Integration, Adding a

> *The blended family, more common in society than the nuclear family, develops in ways that defy the life cycle model of change.*

New Baby, Stepchildren Leaving Home, and Eldercare (pp. 38–47). Although researchers have recognized the three later stages, the Initial Integration transition has been the focus for most researchers who study blended families. These studies tend to describe "samples of dominant-culture, middle-class, post-divorce, and remarried households in which the minor children reside rather than visit" (p. 38). The tasks that the family manages during this stage include grieving losses from the disruption of the prior family and being open to a new type of family. The stability/change dialectic is therefore likely to be prevalent at this time. Accordingly, boundaries are realigned "to find an appropriate place for the stepparent(s) in the leadership subsystem" as older children are relieved from their leadership responsibilities and privileges (p. 38). The difficulty of managing this transition will depend, in part, on the length of time that the child has been in the leadership role and also the degree of security that he or she feels with the biological parent. Related to these changes are ambiguities of stepparent and stepchild roles, adjusting between residential and visiting households, and stepparents without children acquiring parenting skills. The development of the conjugal relationship, with issues of intimacy, division of labor, childcare, and decision making, is also paramount during this initial integration. Finally, sibling relationships and co-parent relationships require "acceptance of the constant changes in household composition as children move between households" (p. 41). Each of these changes could be managed from a dialectical approach using strategies of selection, separation, neutralization, and reformulation.

A dialectical approach to development also shows how the blended family departs from the norm established by a life cycle approach. During courtship, for example, at least one of the partners is a parent with a history of a prior relationship. In such situations, there will be tension between marital and parental relationships. From their research with stepfamily members, Cissna, Cox, and Bochner (1989) found that "a natural tension, or 'relationship dialectic,' seems to exist for the adults between maintaining a spousal relationship—their own marriage—and simultaneously developing a relationship with one or more children" (p. 8). Furthermore, "The process of change or reorganization within the stepfamily depends on the successful management of this relationship dialectic" (p. 8).

A family may choose to manage the tension between the marital and parental relationship through selection, by ignoring the children in favor of focusing on the marriage. Selection will create a different developmental outcome than that of a family adopting other strategies of management. Stepfamilies often use separation, for instance, as they divide their time between complex biological and step relational needs. Or a couple may choose to make special time for themselves on the weekends while focusing on parenting tasks during the week. If a blended family attempts to do some things the same as before but also adopts new traditions, they are exhibiting neutralization as a way to deal with and direct their change. The reformulation of the stability/change dialectic may take the form of a reframe, in which the family attends to what is new in the old and what is old in the new as their way of embracing its contradictory force. For example, a married couple may emphasize how performing their daily routines gives them an opportunity to discover new issues in a routine way.

> *If a blended family attempts to do some things the same as before but also adopts new traditions, they are exhibiting neutralization as a way to deal with and direct their change.*

In their attempt to develop an understanding of blended family development, Crocker-Lakness and Sabourin (2000) adopt a seven-stage model. Their model extends the earlier work of Papernow (1984) and reflects stepfamilies' processes as they set goals, determine parental limits, create stepparent bonds, blend family rules, and reset relations in their binuclear families (Crocker-Lakness & Sabourin, 2000, pp. 1–2). The model is suggestive of how structural diversity affects family development, creating unique but not necessarily deficient patterns. It also allows us to conceptualize the nonnuclear structure as normative for some families.

Stepfamily Development Among Married Couples

Confusion. The first stage of stepfamily development is characterized by confusion. As members of a stepfamily attempt to make their new family work, they face the dialectic of the ideal and the real. Ideally, they may imagine that the stepfamily will be just like their nuclear family and that it will heal the wounds from their experience of being broken. At the same time, however, they must face a cultural stereotype of stepfamilies that is negative (Crocker-Lakness & Sabourin, 2000; Hughes & Schroeder, 1997). While parents may fantasize that the new family is a place of rescue for themselves and their children, the children may wish for their biological parents to get back together and for the new marriage to fail (Cissna, Bochner, & Cox, 1989). As a result of these conflicting expectations and the gap between the imagined and real stepfamily experience, the family's initial blending produces much confusion.

Conflict. During the next phase of stepfamily formation, confusion turns into conflict. Dialectically, there may be a contradictory desire for both assimilation and distance that results in an attitude of "We're glad you're here, but don't come in" (Crocker-Lakness, 1996, p. 3). At this stage, boundaries between the stepparent and the biological parent are likely to emerge and, "unable to break into the strong bonds between biological parent and children, the stepparent feels jealous, resentful, and inadequate" (p. 3). In turn, the biological parent may "interpret the stepparent's difficulty in being assimilated into the family as a lack of interest or effort" (p. 3).

Thus, this stage may produce a sense of isolation and even despair about the state of the new family.

Awareness. The awareness phase develops as clarity sets in and both stepparent and biological parent begin to realize the pressures of their situation. The biological parent, for instance, "comes to understand that developing an intimate relationship with the new spouse requires some exclusion of the children and the establishment of new family rules" (Crocker-Lakness, 1996, p. 3). Although "honest and clear communication is still not possible . . . the confusion and sense of failure of the earlier stages grows into an ability to accept some responsibility" (p. 3). Papernow (1984) found that, to get to this stage, families take from two to three years. This means that family members must be patient as they develop some awareness and understanding of the new family process.

Mobilization. The insight from the previous step results in mobilization at stage four. Here, the stepparent may begin to voice his or her realizations and make some demands on the children and the spouse. At issue during this stage is "whether the biological subsystem will continue to be primary or whether the stepfamily will restructure itself around the relationship between the biological parent and the stepparent" (Crocker-Lakness, 1996, p. 4). New rules for the stepfamily may emerge that differ from the rules of the prior family and that differ from the rules of the noncustodial household. As they give voice to their perceptions and needs, couples can begin to make joint decisions about themselves and their new family.

Bonding. The decisions made at step four are activated in the next stage. The family develops a sense of shared meaning and may act out a contract that includes "some of the old ways of doing things while creating new rituals, rules and boundaries"

(Crocker-Lakness, 1996, p. 4). As a result, a new degree of bonding may occur, leading to the intimacy of the next stage.

Intimacy. During the intimacy stage, members of the blended family experience a new type of "authenticity in their relationships" (Crocker-Lakness, 1996, p. 4). They see themselves as valid, as their new structure has evolved to a point where it can replace the old one. Their reality as a blended family is more familiar and memories of the "way it used to be" fade. The step-couple experiences a new solidarity at this stage and is more respected by the children as a legitimate couple.

Let it be. From the intimacy of the prior phase, the blended family, now truly "blended," replaces their sense of "making it happen" with "letting it be" (Crocker-Lakness, 1996, p. 5). Stepparents accept that they may not be a "full" parent but still recognize the importance of their "step" roles. Biological parents let go of their need for overinvolvement with their children, "which was so comforting immediately following the break-up of the original family" (p. 5). At this stage, families are more equipped to deal with the problems that arise as they share their own history of joint decision making. As a result, "the identity of 'stepfamily' can now recede into the background where it offers a grounding of strength for the family's successful handling of problems" (p. 5).

If the development of the nuclear family-of-origin is disrupted through death or divorce, making it a single-parent family, and then remarriage occurs, creating a blended family, the old nuclear "map" will not suffice as a guide for the family's development and may create disappointment and confusion. Instead, if a map of the seven stages of blended family development as outlined by Papernow (1984) and Crocker-Lakness (1996) is provided, the family will be better prepared and have a much better guide to follow, allowing them a better chance of success in reaching their destination.

> *If the development of the nuclear family-of-origin is disrupted through death or divorce, making it a single-parent family, and then remarriage occurs, creating a blended family, the old nuclear "map" will not suffice as a guide for the family's development and may create disappointment and confusion.*

Development is also going to vary when a same-sex couple forms a lasting, intimate relationship. To begin, the public expression of "couple-ness," which is integral to premarital bonding, is forbidden by the culture at large and perhaps even by the family-of-origin and close friends. This means that same-sex couples must court in a nontraditional way, paying great attention to the public/private dialectic.

Stepfamily Development Among Same-Sex Couples

For the same-sex couple, making the decision that the other is "marriageable" does not lead to marriage in the same sense as it can for heterosexual couples. Because the union of same-sex couples is not legally recognized, the very experience of being homosexual can affect family development. In fact, according to Smith and Jones (1999), the gay or lesbian person undertakes three major tasks that are unique to them as a result of their homosexual identity. First, they themselves must recognize that their sexuality is not like that of the majority. They must then be honest with not only themselves but others about their sexual orientation, the process known as *coming out*. If they are thus honest, they may confront both heterosexism and homophobia from their families, from their peers, and even from strangers. It is more than likely in our culture today that they will experience an anti-gay bias and active discouragement from living openly as gay or lesbian. In the United States, at this writing, we not only discourage gays and lesbians from living their lives in complete honestly, we prohibit their forming a legally recognized marital union with members of the same sex.

As a result of the differential experiences of gays or lesbians in an anti-gay society such as the United States, the development of their marital and familial lives will deviate from that outlined in the nuclear map. In their book *On the Road to Same-Sex Marriage,* Smith and Jones propose a more suitable model to describe development in the homosexual or dual-orientation family (1999, pp. 15–16). The stages they include in the model are blending, nesting, maintaining, building, releasing, and renewing. Quite briefly, their characteristics follow.

- During the *blending stage*, which occurs during the first year of the relationship, a desire to be together and sexual activity are both high.
- During *nesting*, which occurs during the second and third years, the main relationship issues revolve around building a home, establishing compatibility, and also ambivalence about the relationship.
- The *maintenance stage*, covering the fourth and fifth years, is characterized by dissatisfaction and conflict.
- The *building stage*, during the sixth through tenth years, is one in which independence is high and individual stresses emerge.
- From the eleventh to the twentieth years, couples go through the *releasing stage*, assuming trust, stability, and comfort in the relationship.
- For couples who are together for twenty or more years, the *renewing stage* occurs. Here, couples restore romance and achieve financial and emotional security.

Although a description of these stages is based on speculation and limited data, the model itself shows how structure and culture influence family development.

In general, the stages reflect how same-sex couples tend to form a bond more quickly than others, given that they have extreme pressure from the public/private dialectical tension to remain in hiding and suppress their desires to express their love publicly in the same ways heterosexual couples can. The quickness of the intimate bond formation means that same-sex couples tend to nest, or move in together, quickly. They then take time to build their relationship, letting go of their fears and renewing the bonds that may have been broken with their families-of-origin. Because their marriages are not legally recognized, same-sex couples must be especially creative in developing their relationship through these early stages. They will run into roadblocks if they attempt to adopt children, but other procreative means are available to same-sex couples wishing to become parents and raise children. The children that are born and raised in same-sex unions will face challenges unlike the challenges of children raised in heterosexual homes.

> *Because their marriages are not legally recognized, same-sex couples must be especially creative in developing their relationship through these early stages.*

A family's appreciation of diversity, of all families in all of their various structures and cultures and of the attitudes taken toward diverse families, may be more critical to the family's development than its structure is. That said, any family, regardless of its structural and cultural variations, can exhibit both functional and dysfunctional patterns.

> *A family's appreciation of diversity, of all families in all of their various structures and cultures and of the attitudes taken toward diverse families, may be more critical to the family's development than its structure is.*

When managing the dialectical tensions inherent in family life, some families adopt more developmentally sound practices than others. Still, it is likely that any given family is not all functional or all dysfunctional. Patterns more likely exist along a continuum, with some being more or less functional at a given place and time. A given pattern is more or less functional, then, dependent on its chronotopical context, and it can be considered as families exhibit diversity in their functionality.

In the next two chapters, we will explore common dysfunctional elements in family life (i.e., the "dark side") and how families can functionally resolve their difficulties (i.e., "living in the light"). Thus, we move toward a way of empowering family development by finding the spirit that transcends all structural and cultural manifestations.

6

Functional Diversity in the Family

The Dark Side

Given a dialectical approach to family life, there is no such thing as a purely functional or a purely dysfunctional family. The embracing stance of the dialectic considers the functional and dysfunctional to be *chronotopically connected*. This means that dysfunctional and functional are relative to a time and place, with fluid meaning attached by any given family member. As a result, it is more correct to speak of a family as functional *and* dysfunctional instead of functional *or* dysfunctional. Interactional and praxical patterns are relatively constructive or destructive, and their meaning will change over time.

Contextually, society must accept that the ideal family, one that is purely functional, does not exist. The real/ideal dialectic exists as a dynamic that will constantly disrupt harmony, making the realization of the ideal a temporal condition rather than a permanent state. In their discussion of family ideals, Stafford and Dainton (1994) assert that:

> The American culture is filled with myths concerning what the family is and should be. The most pervasive myth is that there is such a thing as a normal family. This normal family takes the form of a white, middle-class group consisting of a first- and only-time legally married, heterosexual couple, 1.8 children and (of course) a family pet, all of whom interact in the idealistic manner of utopian normalcy (pp. 260–261).

Stafford and Dainton challenge the assumptions behind these myths as "highly skewed in several ways" (p. 261). First, as emphasized throughout this book, "numerous family structures currently exist" and it is estimated that eventually "stepfamilies will outnumber all other family forms." In turn, they regard structures as contributing to either the health or the destruction of the family, although they recognize that "variations in structure and co-cultural interaction patterns are equally functional and normal." The myth also affects the expectations of family members and the researchers who study them. "For example, co-cultural family members often internalize the values of the White, middle-class ideal and evaluate their own families as lacking." Even "normal" families who match the demographics of mainstream social values "gauge their families against the supposedly optimal model and hence perceive their families as deficient" (p. 261).

Mothers, for example, are often given either praise or blame for family outcomes. In her book *Mother Nature: A History of Mothers, Infants, and Natural Selection*, primate expert Sarah Blaffer Hrdy (1999) challenges the commonly held view of mothers as innately more nurturing, comforting, and caring than fathers. She goes on to say that, although we know what a "good" mother is, we do not know where to find her. Hrdy claims that the good mother isn't just missing in action but that she never existed. As a challenge to evolutionary biology, Hrdy's book explains how selective forces have shaped maternal behaviors over thousands of years. Whereas some argue, then, that the ideal mother is a morally correct creature who rises above her human limitations, others would argue that because of her human limitations, such an ideal mother will never materialize. This means that those who survive are mothers who can adapt to dialectical forces that include both building up and tearing down of family relationships.

Communication has the power to create and to destroy relationships within the family. Another myth of the American family, however, is that love and harmony will prevail. But according to a dialectical notion of human

> *Another myth of the American family is that love and harmony will prevail.*

interaction, both adverse and supportive patterns "permeate routine family interaction at all levels: the marital relationship, the parent-child relationship, the sibling relationship, and the family as a whole" (Stafford & Dainton, 1994, p. 262).

In fact, in a study on divorced spouses' accounts of why their marriages failed, Harvey, Wells, and Alvarez (1978) identified a set of four emergent themes:

1. the chronic failings of one spouse (e.g., alcoholism, abuse, inability to maintain steady employment),

2. growing apart (i.e., common ground shrinks and nothing new takes its place),

3. the marriage was wrong from the start (i.e., one of the spouses knew they married the wrong person for the wrong reason), and

4. poor communication (i.e., couples could not develop a sense of shared meaning or complete the interactional tasks of early marriage such as co-defining reality, integrating expectations, and organizing the relationship).

Although the Harvey, Wells, and Alvarez study was conducted a number of years ago, the themes are equally applicable to explain the attributions we make about "failed" marriages today. From a dialectical view, however, the failure of a marriage may be an inevitable feature of its contradictory demands for stability and change, autonomy and connection, expressiveness and protectiveness, and instrumentality and affection. What can sustain a family through the contradictory demands and the appearances of failure are their praxical improvisations. In other words, the ways in which families embrace and resist dialectical demands will affect their trajectory into the future. And, although permanence is—along with fidelity—a central value to the American marriage, it is not a dialectical possibility. There may be a permanently changing marriage that survives and grows through its changes via praxical improvisation that embraces the whole, but a marriage that both never changes and lasts forever is a dialectic impossibility.

> *The ways in which families embrace and resist dialectical demands will affect their trajectory into the future.*

And yet, more often than not, it is just such a prescription that is given to couples as they enter marriage. Couples are well prepared for the honeymoon and "bliss" of marriage, which usually does not last as a constant state beyond the honeymoon, but are really never prepared for the disillusionment that enters along with daily life beyond the wedding. Media create and perpetuate false expectations, encouraging idealized notions of marriage as a source of completion and bliss.

By always trying to do the right thing in marriage according to how it is culturally defined at the moment, couples can actually harm their relationship. For his therapeutic work with couples, Charny (1986) developed the Profile of Marital Functioning tool, designed to discover "a broad, many-faceted, but still concise picture of a couple's strengths and weaknesses" (p. 571). A desire to totally avoid weakness can become a weakness in itself, as it discourages humility and an openness to change. As Charny, who adopts "a dialectical approach to the interplays of strengths and weaknesses," explains,

> At no point are weaknesses forever conquered; in fact, to the extent that an individual or couple perceives themselves as having overcome all their weaknesses, the dialectical approach implies that a new form of breakdown then becomes more probable. The dialectical principle leads us to a new appreciation of weaknesses, not only as existentially inevitable (so if you can't beat them, join them), but also creates a welcome partnership in oppositions of strengths and weaknesses that sets in motion a creative process of potential growth. When the dialectical process is suppressed or avoided, such as by sameness and doing everything "well and correctly," there is the failure to grow that therapists have come to see in couples and families (pp. 574–575).

When couples can recognize how an insistence on developing only their strengths can itself become a weakness, they open themselves to a wider variety in praxical improvisations. When couples consistently attempt to select strengths over weaknesses through suppression or avoidance, they are limited from the growth that the use of other strategies, such as temporal separation, could enable. For example, if couples used separation, temporally focusing on strengths at one time (for instance, during the work week) and weaknesses during special problem-solving sessions (perhaps during weekly family meetings on Sundays), it is likely that they will be more aware of the dynamic interplay of their strengths and weaknesses.

Sometimes, however, couples choose to ignore their weakness for the sake of developing their strengths. Charny (1986) discusses how couples who are very adept at parenting may ignore

A desire to totally avoid weakness can become a weakness in itself, as it discourages humility and an openness to change.

their own intimate relationship; as such, their emphasis on parenting may become an obsessive way to block the increasing pain that they feel over their lack of intimacy. As he explains, there is an "inherent possibility of overdoing any type of experience to the point where the quality of an initially lovely experience will be transformed to something difficult and less attractive" (p. 575). In other words, just as

> "too much" changes the quality of what one is doing for the worse, being too involved and invested in what one does best generally also means not paying enough attention to one's poor functioning and weaknesses, so that there is less energy available to correct them, or at least to acknowledge these weaknesses responsibly (p. 575).

The dialectical approach encourages an honest acknowledgment of both weaknesses and strengths, recognizing their transformative nature. Depending on how contradictions are managed, an apparent strength (such as never having conflicts to keep harmony among family members) can turn into a weakness (never expressing discontent can result in stagnation). Conversely, through recognition, an apparent weakness can become a strength. This challenges the societal emphasis on functional or dysfunctional families. For a time in the early 1990s, it was quite fashionable to have come from a dysfunctional family, and dysfunctional mothers were found to be the cause of most adult-children ailments, from low self-esteem to drug addiction. Without downplaying the fact that some families exhibit more healthy patterns whereas other tend to be more destructive, all families are, to some extent, both functional and dysfunctional. As a way to illustrate how a dialectical approach can apply to a discussion of the dark side of family life, this chapter explores the impact of alcoholism, abuse, and divorce on family dynamics. To provide a holistic coverage of family life, the next chapter will illustrate how many families manage their darkness through the light of spirituality.

❖ THE IMPACT OF ALCOHOLISM ON THE FAMILY

As paradoxical as it seems, many a child of an alcoholic becomes an alcoholic. And if they don't become alcoholic, they marry an alcoholic or a person with some other compulsive addictive personality disorder.

—John Bradshaw, *The Family*, 1988, p. 88

High stress, lack of predictability, and powerlessness are all part of the environment for the family living with a chemically dependent person.

—Stephanie Abbott, *Codependency:*
A Second Hand Life, 1985, p. 3

Cessation of drinking is but the first step away from a highly strained, abnormal condition. A doctor said to us, "Years of living with an alcoholic is almost sure to make any wife or child neurotic. The entire family is, to some extent, ill."

—*Big Book of Alcoholic Anonymous*, 1976, p. 122

Alcoholism as a Disease

For many years, we considered alcoholism a moral issue caused by a lack of willpower within the alcoholic. We know that families with alcoholic members become sick themselves as they seek to cover for the alcoholic, via enabling, or try to cure the alcoholic through pressure, threats, and coercion. The more a family attempts to control the alcoholic, however, the more the alcoholic's disease controls and dominates the life of the family. We now consider alcoholism a family disease. Although a family would normally seek help from the medical community to treat other diseases, such as diabetes or cancer, that a family member might have, most families try to treat alcoholism privately and without medical intervention. The myth that alcoholism is treatable through the willpower of the alcoholic contributes to the shame and demoralization of alcoholics and their families as their attempts to treat themselves through willpower alone consistently fail.

> *We know that families with alcoholic members become sick themselves as they seek to cover for the alcoholic, via enabling, or try to cure the alcoholic through pressure, threats, and coercion.*

When willpower does not work, the alcoholic continues to drink. The drinking is a symptom of the disease of alcoholism and a personality that is creative but immature, passionate yet impulsive, selfish yet generous—in other words, full of contradictions. Dialectically, the alcoholic personality feels the pressures of contradiction more profoundly than most. To manage the tension, the alcoholic drinks. The drinking can be seen, then, as a selection strategy for avoidance of the dialectical strains of family life and the inability to cope with them. Using only willpower to cure the disease of alcoholism is akin to trying to fix a broken leg with a Band-Aid. The problem lies deep within; surface measures to fix it are fruitless.

The Family's Reactions to Their Alcoholic Member

The family's reactions to their alcoholic member are often control-based. This means that family members try to get the alcoholic spouse or offspring to change, to quit drinking. Trying to solve the problem through control, however, tends to feed the problem instead. A control-based response to alcoholism is futile in terms of its curative value. Although logical, it grossly underestimates the power of the disease to destroy not only the alcoholic but all who are in his or her path. Health professionals are beginning to see alcoholism as a "family systems based problem" (Pardeck, 1991, p. 342) having widespread repercussions for all of its members. Many contend that "this dysfunctional patterning will change only if the family is willing to enter treatment" (p. 343).

Alcoholism and the Family's Developmental Patterns

Alcoholism has far-reaching consequences on the family's developmental patterns. For example, in a study of college-age alcoholics, it was found that young abusers are often highly connected (enmeshed) with their family of origin. Their alcohol use postpones the necessary process of separation and preserves "the dysfunctional alignments of the troubled family system" (Pardeck, 1991, p. 343). Thus, alcoholism affects the family's management of the dependence/independence interactional dialectic by prolonging dependency of children on parents and ignoring the need for separation. Developmental stresses that occur for late adolescent and college-age children, such as awakened sexuality and identity crises, are intensified in alcoholic families, who often deal with crises via denial. Through selection, family members attempt to avoid the abysmal qualities of alcoholism and engage exclusively in certainty-seeking activities.

Researchers disagree about the extent to which alcoholism is genetically or culturally based. So far, researchers take the stance that alcoholism is a disease that is not caused by cultural factors. Stressful family and social conditions might cause drinking, but such external factors cannot cause the emergence of the disease

> *Through selection, family members attempt to avoid the abysmal qualities of alcoholism and engage exclusively in certainty-seeking activities.*

of alcoholism. That is not to say that alcoholism is devoid of both influencing and being influenced by familial and societal factors. In fact, a number of studies have examined how alcoholism is related to various outcomes for family members.

Studies of Alcoholism and Families

Menees (1997)

Menees (1997) studied the relationship between adult children of alcoholics' (ACA) self-esteem and their parents' alcoholism. Although the stereotype of ACA is one of depression and severe relational problems, Menees's study sought to find moderator variables that could account for the variations in ACAs' self-esteem. In other words, rejecting the stereotype as an overly simplistic account of ACAs, Menees examined how alcoholism affects self-esteem variably across children.

To do so, she identified how the resources that ACAs have at their disposal can create vulnerability or protection as they cope with parental alcoholism. Vulnerability factors increase the negative potential of alcoholism on a child's self-esteem. In an environment where praxical improvisation manifests as criticism and denial of feelings—where judgment is consistently selected over acceptance—the negative impact of alcoholism will be greater. Protective factors that reduce the impact of stressors such as alcoholism include problem-solving ability, humor, social support, and the ability to express feelings. *Ventilation* or the expression of feelings can act as a moderator between parental alcoholism and ACA self-esteem; its impact, however, is not unequivocal. Although Menees found that "being a low ventilator may put children of alcoholics more at risk" (p. 14), parental alcoholism is not a direct cause of a child's ability to express feelings.

Knowles and Schroeder (1990)

Another study examined the personalities of sons of alcoholics (Knowles & Schroeder, 1990). The association between being an ACA and having mental illness (such as hypochondria, depression, and hysteria) was again found to be unclear. Assuming that existing differences come from both genetic loading and the home environment (i.e., nature *and* nurture), the researchers speculate that, over time, the neurotic tendencies will compound into a consistently negative influence. The compounding of negative influence can become, in turn, a risk factor predicting the child's own foray into alcoholism. Risk is the statistical probability that a specific outcome (usually negative) will occur at a later date. Thus, a number of factors operate together with genetics to exacerbate an ACA's risk for alcoholism. These include the rearing environments of school, peers, and family, and how each treats alcohol.

Clark, Kirisci, and Moss (1998)

While we estimate that one eighth, or 12.5%, of children are children of alcoholics (with 77% of these having alcoholic fathers, 10% having alcoholic mothers, and 13% having both parents as alcoholics), the inheritance of alcoholism is seen to be the result of a complex biopsychosocial process. "Being the child of a parent with substance abuse disorders (SUD) increases liability for substance use and psychopathology" (Clark, Kirisci, & Moss, 1998, p. 561). Specifically, such children have more conduct disorders, more antisocial behaviors, more negative affect, and more mental disorders than children without SUD history. Although it cannot be said that alcoholism will have a certain impact, we can identity those with high and low risk.

A Clinical Approach to Alcoholism

Although these studies and similar other studies attempt to explore the complex patterns of influence that alcoholism has on the family, they fail to identify the many subtle qualities and outcomes from living in an alcoholic home. The outcomes emerge gradually and have differential impact during various life stages, requiring longitudinal study.

A clinical approach to alcoholism focuses more on environmental than genetic factors. As Bradshaw (1988) states, "It's clear that as children of alcoholics, we are not just reacting to the drinking of the alcoholic. What we're reacting to are the relational issues, the anger, the control issues, the emotional unavailability of the addict" (p. 89). The relational issues that emerge across alcoholic families are strikingly similar, as are the patterns of response that they exhibit in their attempts to manage the dialectical contradictions imposed by these issues.

The roles played by children in alcoholic families reflect how, to survive, they "cut off from many of their feelings" and perform in rigid, predictable ways. The roles include The Hero, The Caretaker, and The Scapegoat. To illustrate how the roles function, consider the following examples:

> In an alcoholic family one child will be a Hero because the family system needs some dignity. If the family system has no warmth, one child will become the emotional Caretaker and be warm and loving to everyone. If the system is ravaged with unexpressed anger and pain, one child will become the Scapegoat and act out all the anger and pain. In every case the person playing the role gives up his own unique selfhood. In dysfunctional families, the individual exists to keep the system in balance. (Bradshaw, 1988, p. 77)

From the same descriptions of role enactments in alcoholic families, it is easy to see how the roles can act as praxical improvisations to manage contradictions as they manifest in the alcoholic family. Bradshaw (1988) explains the function of the roles as "necessitated by the covert or overt needs of the family as a system" (p. 77). From a dialectical view, the covert and overt needs that emerge from the tensions of stability/change and autonomy/connection can never be permanently "balanced." In the systems sense of balance, homeostasis is implied, in which a family comes to a resting place and dialectical contradictions are overcome. "Contradiction is not regarded as something to bemoan or extinguish," however. "Contradiction is instead embraced on its own terms" (Baxter & Montgomery, 1996, p. 60). Whereas a more functional response means "learning to live on 'friendly terms' with paradox, contradiction, and multivocality" (p. 60), some families, including those with the disease of alcoholism, tend to exhibit patterns that "are characterized by limited functionality" and a failure to accept their own contradictory nature (p. 60).

Two specific praxical patterns with limited functionality that emerge in alcoholic families are denial and disorientation. The denial strategy "represents an effort to subvert, obscure, and deny the presence of a contradiction by legitimating only one dialectical pole to the virtual exclusion of the other poles" (Baxter & Montgomery, 1996, p. 61). Denial is a form of a selection strategy because the family accepts only one element of their situation as real. As they attempt to survive the relational issues presented by alcoholism, family members lock into rigid roles that deny change. Thus, while they embrace stability, trying to maintain a rigid routine through enactment of these roles, even in the midst of chaos, they do so by holding back the sands of time. Because denial creates only an illusion that "all is well," the alcoholic family will continue to deteriorate (a form of change).

The point with denial is that a family cannot heal from a disease that it fails to acknowledge. Hence, denial is a powerfully covert way to attempt management of the tension between stability and change. In essence, it says, "If we don't acknowledge the alcoholism, it doesn't really exist; it may even go away if we

> *As they attempt to survive the relational issues presented by alcoholism, family members lock into rigid roles that deny change.*

ignore it for long enough." Although the pain of alcoholism makes denial an attractive alternative, as a modus operandi, like any praxical pattern, it will eventually have to give way to a strategy that recognizes the whole and contradictory nature of the polarity. Many times, however, the alcoholic family goes on to bitter destruction before it can surrender to this truth.

Another pattern with limited functionality is "disorientation." "This response involves a fatalistic attitude in which contradictions are regarded as inevitable, negative, and unresponsive to praxical change" (Baxter & Montgomery, 1996, p. 62). Instead of recognizing that one's response to dialectical contradictions transforms it into the next reality, those who choose disorientation refuse to see anything but confusion and defeat as legitimate ways to act toward their situation. In alcoholic families, spouses and children often attempt to repeat their patterns again and again, knowing that, although they did not get the desired response on previous occasions (the alcoholic did not stop drinking),

> *In alcoholic families, spouses and children often attempt to repeat their patterns again and again, knowing that, although they did not get the desired response on previous occasions (the alcoholic did not stop drinking), "This time will be different."*

"This time will be different." Spouses might know deep inside that hiding bottles will not keep the alcoholic from drinking, but they do it anyway, hoping to change reality.

Baxter and Montgomery (1996) note how similar disorientation is to the notion of *undesired repetitive patterns* (URPs), introduced some years ago by Cronen, Pearce, and Snavely (1979). The URP occurs when one's intentions and behaviors are inconsistent. For example, if a couple is used to fighting over their child's alcoholism, blaming instead of owning the problem, they may become stuck "through a passive acceptance that often becomes manifest in the ambiguity of mixed messages" (Baxter & Montgomery, 1996, p. 62). In other words, they cannot directly confront their situation because their communication patterns produce only confusion, or what some clinicians refer to as *crazy-making behavior.*

Disorientation is often based on disjunctive verbal and non-verbal messages. Verbally, a family may appear to express affection for each other, but nonverbally they express a desire for distance (Baxter & Montgomery, 1996). Thus, the autonomy/connection dialectic can be managed through disorientation, in which family members are simultaneously told to "come close" and to "go away." This paradoxical injunction is familiar to families with an alcoholic member. The alcoholic is caught in an intimate relationship with the alcohol and is unavailable to family members in all but the most superficial way. To compensate, spouses and children may become overly available, not out of a desire for true intimacy but as a reaction to an intense fear of abandonment (Bradshaw, 1988). As a result, the management of the autonomy/connection dialectic, when met through disorientation, creates a confused state of over- or underinvolvement masquerading as intimacy.

The *what's-the-use?* feeling behind disorientation can be reinforced through the family's praxical improvisations. Although they may mistake the results of their interactions as confirmation for their beliefs in futility and hopelessness, alcoholic families do have

> *Although they may mistake the results of their interactions as confirmation for their beliefs in futility and hopelessness, alcoholic families do have choices that can enable them to change in a direction of healing.*

choices that can enable them to change in a direction of healing. As one woman says,

> I hid his bottles, and looked for the ones he had hidden. I spent hours putting water in the vodka, and marking levels of alcohol on the bottles. Looking back, I can see how point-less it all was, but it seemed important at the time. I used to pace the floor crying, my mind so blank I couldn't think. I rehearsed what I would say to him, and imagined what he would answer. I was sure if I could plan the right words, I could reach him. (Abbott, 1985, p. 2)

As a group, families of alcoholics exhibit predictable styles of management. Although we have discussed the less functional improvisational alternatives to manage contradiction, we know that some families will learn to approach alcoholism in more functional ways. In the next chapter, we examine these more functional responses. First, however, we turn our attention to another dark side of family life, that of domestic abuse.

❖ DOMESTIC VIOLENCE

The presence of abuse between spouses, parents and children, and siblings in a family contradicts the myth of the family as "a 'haven in a heartless world'" (Stafford & Dainton, 1994, p. 263). Although some conceptualizations of normal family functioning are restricted to constructive traits—such as respecting, support-ing, trusting, and listening—such levels of optimal functioning cannot be held constant. As Harvey, Wells, and Alvarez explain, "From a dialogical point of view, the positive and the negative co-exist in social behavior" (1978, p. 260). The dialogical approach recognizes that "normal family interaction is a paradox of conflicting messages of support and hurt," and all families sometimes manifest patterns that are "less than optimal"

(Stafford & Dainton, 1994, p. 260). As a result, drawing the line between acceptable shortcomings in family interactions and actual abuse is not often simple or straightforward.

Because physical abuse is easier to see and measure, it has received the most attention from researchers and policymakers. A broken arm can provide unambiguous evidence that a parent or a spouse has crossed the line between acceptable behavior and abuse. As a result, the law can determine that physical abuse is a violation of another's rights and punish the offender accordingly. Other instances of abuse, however, are not so obvious. How is emotional abuse to be measured, counted, or seen, especially by objective observers? Consider the following definition of emotional abuse:

> Emotional abuse is behavior that does violence to the very heart of a relationship—to the emotional connection between two people. Though it is not physically violent, emotional abuse wounds both victimizer and victim, as well as the relationship between them. Every relationship has moments of anger, distance, and upset. In healthy relationships, these ruptures are repaired by apologies and changes that address the causes of the hurtful behavior. In contrast, the wounds of emotionally abusive relationships are not repaired, and their damage accumulates over time. (Thompson, 1993, p. 1)

Furthermore, the presence of abuse is not limited to any particular structural or cultural family configuration. Although certain structures have been identified as posing a higher risk for abuse, we often overlook the interaction of the structure with other socioeconomic conditions. For instance, although many studies report that "child abuse occurs at higher rates in stepfamilies than in natal families . . . there are many unanswered questions about the accuracy of this claim and its causes" (Giles-Sims, 1997, p. 215). In her review of these studies, Giles-Sims concludes that to claim validity, "we must identify which children are at higher risk rather than stereotype a whole family structure" (p. 226). Factors that correlate with abuse, such as low incomes, high conflict, drug and alcohol dysfunctions, and isolation, may be problems that "self-select into stepfamilies at higher rates than natal families through divorce and remarriage" (p. 223). Although she finds that girls in stepfamilies are at higher risk for sexual abuse, she is careful to warn "that not all children in stepfamilies are at risk" (p. 227).

Abuse in the family does not limit itself to any particular time or place. In fact, many families experience abuse as part of their mundane, communicative reality. It is in the day-to-day routine that the "murky playing field of the dark elements of family interaction" is most likely to appear (Stafford & Dainton, 1994, p. 261).

> *Abuse in the family does not limit itself to any particular time or place. In fact, many families experience abuse as part of their mundane, communicative reality.*

Prior to the 1970s, abuse went unreported in the academic journals. During the early 1970s, some early reports of child abuse were made, yet the implication was that child abuse was rare and limited to a certain form of pathology. As reports of wife abuse became increasingly common in the late 1970s and then exploded in the 1980s, family scholars and practitioners began to identify more garden-variety types of abuse. With the prevalence of abuse patterns emerging through today, it is apparent that many families experience it as a part of daily life. Abuse is not always sensational. In fact, that which is subtler and more deeply imbedded into the interaction patterns of family members may, in the long run, be even more damaging than the glaringly obvious occasional physical beating. There are laws to prevent family members from outright physical cruelty (although the laws are only more or less effective depending on the climate of enforcement), yet there is nowhere to turn when abuse is verbal or emotional.

Early studies of abuse focused on the patterns surrounding an abusive episode (e.g., being severely beaten). They discovered structural similarities across physically abusive incidents that husbands inflicted on their wives. Each inci-

Abuse is not always sensational. In fact, that which is subtler and more deeply imbedded into the interaction patterns of family members may, in the long run, be even more damaging than the glaringly obvious occasional physical beating.

dent consisted of a period of tension, followed by an explosion into violence, and ending with contrition (Walker, 1979). In a study that compared the routine interactions of abusive and nonabusive families rather than the abusive ones per se, Sabourin and Stamp (1995) found that the differences permeated a wide range of nonabusive experiences. That is, even when the couples were discussing seemingly neutral topics selected by the researcher to minimize the potential for conflict, they still had trouble agreeing and seemed to be fighting for control of each other's perceptions. The nonabusive couples, on the other hand, cooperated with each other in their discussion of a neutral topic.

In a more finely grained examination of the conversational data gathered from the abusive and nonabusive couples for the Sabourin and Stamp (1995) study, Sabourin (1995) applied a relational control analysis to locate quantitative evidence for the patterns of negative reciprocity that appeared at a qualitative level. Negative reciprocity, which occurs when an aversive behavior on the part of one family member is met with a similarly aversive behavior on the part of another, has been found to be characteristic of abusive couples in the few studies that have examined their conversations (Cordova, Jacobson, Gottman, Rushe, & Cox, 1993; Gage, 1988; Sabourin, 1995). In all of these studies, "The fact that husbands and wives match verbal aggression with verbal aggression is surprising, given the traditional view of spouse abuse" (Sabourin, 1995, p. 272). The traditional view of spouse abuse reflects a commonly held assumption that men are the aggressors and women the passive victims, thus describing a complementary (i.e., one-up, one-down) relationship. However, when compared to the nonabusive spouses' conversations, both husbands and wives from the abusive couples attempted to be domineering, suggesting that "they may lack the communicative means and/or motivation to repair the impact of aversive behavior" (Sabourin, 1995, p. 272). In other words, neither spouse was willing to accept the other's relational definition. Hence, symmetrical escalation emerged (i.e., each spouse makes one-up moves).

The presence of negative reciprocity can act like a time bomb waiting to explode when conditions are just right. It keeps a couple on edge and provides evidence that they do not agree on how to organize the power dimension of their relationship. Each wants to control the relationship, and neither is willing to compromise. Nonabusive couples, on the other hand, were not as likely to respond to each other through reciprocal behavior. Instead, they built off of each other's conversation and created an agreed-on version of reality to describe their daily routine. These results corroborate the earlier work of Gottman and Krokoff (1989) who report that "negative interaction is much more common in the interaction of unhappily married couples than happily married couples" (p. 47).

Together, these studies provide some evidence to support the idea that abusive families do not exhibit healthy patterns of interaction as a rule and then one day have a sudden outburst of violence. Instead, the whole of their relational patterns is distinctive from those of healthy families who do not exhibit abuse. They seem especially distinctive in terms of the quality of negative reciprocity, indicating an inability to agree at the relational control level of their interaction.

We can view the patterns of emotional, physical, and/or verbal abuse that develop in families as attempts to manage the dialectical tensions of autonomy/connection and stability/change. We recognize that control, for example, is a major factor in the psychology of the abusive male (Sabourin, 2000). Paradoxically, abusive males seek to control their partners and limit their autonomy as a way to cope with the helplessness they experience as a result of not being able to control their partners. This control effort is so central to the battering males' perceptions that programs to treat battering males often as a primary goal teach the men to "discontinue their attempts to control their spouse" (Ventura, Milholland, & Trujillo, 1994, p. 2).

If we see control as a strategy for managing the contradiction of autonomy/connection, it may be a form of selection: Rather than sharing control, one person attempts to take over the other's autonomy. In turn, the pole of connection (enmeshment) is enforced through the abuse. In other words, a male may think to himself, "If I can't control her through other means, I will force her, through violence, to obey me." Obeying is a way to ensure connection as it creates an imbalance of dependency of one spouse on the other. In such a situation, those being controlled are robbed of their autonomy.

We can identify deeply rooted causes of anger and violence as the battering males go through treatment. Because batterers tend to justify and minimize their abuse,

> *Obeying is a way to ensure connection as it creates an imbalance of dependency of one spouse on the other.*

they often blame their spouse and fail to acknowledge their own role in the relationship. To change this, before the state of Florida offers accreditation to treatment programs for batters, it requires that the program teaches its clients that "domestic violence cannot be provoked" (Burnette, 1994). Accredited treatment programs in Florida teach batterers to be responsible for their behavior, no matter what their partner seemingly did to provoke them.

Blaming and minimizing can be seen as ways to select stability over change. If spouses refuse to see their own role in a relational outcome, such as abuse, in essence they are attempting to prevent change. By insisting on a certain course of action and then reinforcing it through terror, batterers try to stabilize their environments. It is one way in which they protect themselves from change, which would disrupt their sense of control. Rather than seeing abuse as strictly evil, if we consider it as a way to manage the uncertainty of family life by eliminating change, its complexity and deeper meaning can emerge. To provide more functional praxical choices to deal with stability and change, programs for battering males emphasize alternative ways to perceive their own and their partner's behavior. Of course, changing the battering male's strategies, with their deeply ingrained reactivity, is not an easy goal to realize.

As we've increased our awareness of the nature of domestic violence, we've also shattered a number of myths (Marshall, 1994). Patterns of domestic violence vary, which challenges the myth that abuse is limited to males aggressing against their female partners. Females also commit acts of violence against their partners and their children. Although some contend that female aggression against male partners is strictly an act of self-defense, there is plenty of evidence to suggest that women also initiate violence (Chandler, 1986; Steinmetz, 1985). It is important to recognize the diversity of abusive patterns so that treatment is not based on a false assumption of homogeneity.

In terms of diversity, researchers have identified a number of domestic violence patterns (Chandler, 1986; Steinmetz, 1985). Some couples are "Saturday night brawlers," becoming abusive only on "special" occasions. It is well documented that on Super Bowl Sunday, a number of women come to the emergency room to be treated for injuries inflicted by their male partners. Saturday night brawlers may also act out abusively after becoming intoxicated at a celebration, such as a wedding, or a holiday such as New Year's eve.

Some couples exhibit a constant, low level of aggression characterized more by verbal than physical abuse. This type of abuse, which is perhaps the most common, is also the most difficult to acknowledge in that families become immune to its presence. Because this garden-variety abuse tends to be less sensational but more frequent, it may not be dramatic enough to attract the attention of the law, the media, or the neighbors. However unacceptable occasional and low-level abuse is, it is distinctive from abuse that becomes chronic, escalating in both intensity and frequency.

Chronic abuse in married heterosexual couples becomes progressively worse. It sometimes begins during courtship but more often waits until after the wedding and almost always catches the spouse by surprise. Incidents of chronic abuse, which start out with the aforementioned phases of tension, explosion, and contrition, eventually become so hateful that the contrition stage disappears. At this point, the relationship consists of interactions that are either tense or violent. As such, chronic abuse is a most frightening and damaging form of domestic violence. It tends to be instrumental (serving as a premeditated means to an end) rather than expressive, and is often deadly. Because of its severity, wives are likely to attempt to leave these relationships but do so at the risk of being stalked, harassed, and eventually murdered by their abusive husbands.

Abuse permeates the fabric of our society, occurring across diverse cultural conditions. Although it has been infrequently studied, abuse between same-sex couples also occurs. Because they are not legally recognized as legitimate unions, protection for gay and lesbian partners in the face of abuse is not guaranteed. Whereas heterosexual couples can rely on the restraining order to keep their abusive family member away from them, restraining orders are not available to victims of abuse in same-sex relationships. But, just as abuse occurs in heterosexual families, it is likely to occur in dual-orientation families.

> *Abuse permeates the fabric*
> *of our society, occurring*
> *across diverse cultural conditions.*

In their study of abuse in lesbian couples, Anderson and Sabourin (1996) conducted a thematic analysis of their conflict narratives. Similar to accounts of heterosexual partners' abusive episodes, we found the lesbians in this study to conflict over issues of relational control. The struggle to gain control over the relationship was attributed to jealousy and to the complexity of the private/public constraints of homosexuality. Because they do not have the same privileges as heterosexual partners to signal their coupleness to others (i.e., openly), normally acceptable public expressions of affection (e.g., holding hands) entail controversy when enacted by lesbians. In turn, this means that lesbian couples have a strong tendency to become overly dependent on each other in that they are constrained from the usual social support network given to heterosexuals. "This intensified dependence upon one's partner can pose intensified problems of separation/individuation" and also strain lesbian couples toward conflict (Anderson & Sabourin, 1996, p. 7).

Although today there are numerous studies that have examined abuse in the family, the rates of abuse are not necessarily different than they were 30 years ago when few studies existed. What has changed, however, a result of the widespread attention from researchers, media, and other societal agents, is that this dark side of family life is now exposed, and we've created laws to formally restrict what was once considered a private matter.

❖ DIVORCE

Although we might wish for families to stay together forever, it is a fact of life that marriage may be a temporary union. Divorce has become a common feature of American family life. Although it may seem that divorce is caused by alcoholism and abuse in the family, the breakup of any marriage is more likely to have multiple and complex reasons. Regardless of a divorce's cause, beyond family members are left to deal with the issues of grief— depression, anger, and fear—that occur after the divorce. Adjustment to the new family structure, which requires great reserves of courage, energy, and flexibility that the family in this ailing form is not likely to have, may expose the dark side of their interaction. Divorce often brings out the very worst in family members as they fight to salvage their shattered identities. Dialectically, we view this dark side as a part of the whole and not as dysfunctional in itself. What can become dysfunctional is the family members' reactions to the demise of their once-intact system.

In their study of communication as mediator of child adjustment to divorce, Linker, Stolberg, and Green (1999) found that "reduced family conflict, consistency in roles and parenting, and limited negative life changes, seem to be particularly important variables in promoting children's adjustment to divorce" (p. 83). Adapting throughout the divorce process takes place over "a series of events, rather than a single event" (p. 84). Thus:

> *Divorce often brings out the very worst in family members as they fight to salvage their shattered identities.*

> Pre- and post-separation parental conflict has many implications for family functioning. Conflict breaks down the communication necessary for co-parenting activities. In addition, parents involved in conflict may model hostility, aggressiveness, and poor problem solving techniques. Children may be caught in difficult positions between hostile parents, and parental conflict may also change the parent/child relationships. Parents become less emotionally available, and one or both parents may be less available physically due to the parental hostilities. In addition, reversals in the parent/child

roles often occur as the parents rely on the children for support. (Linker, Stolberg, and Green, 1999, pp. 85–86)

Divorce changes the boundaries that define who is "in" and who is "out" of the family. As such, we may alter the criteria for inclusion. Whereas a given person was once considered family because of blood ties, after a divorce occurs, that person's status changes unless other functional and interactional bonds exist. Conversely, nonblood neighbors or friends who were not included within family boundaries prior to divorce may enter into the fold through their functional and/or interactional bonds. If divorced parents become involved with support groups, for example, they may establish new bonds with parents in similar situations. As they offer guidance and encouragement, these support people may come to be considered as part of the family.

The impact of divorce lingers into the young adulthood of children because it affects the evolution of their life-course (Amato, 1999). Its impact will vary across adult children, however, in that "the association between stressful life events and developmental outcomes is not always direct or simple" (p. 149). Although they are exposed to a higher level of risk, some will be more resilient than others. "For example, children who must cope with economic hardship are likely to have a more difficult time adjusting to divorce than are children who experience a comfortable post-divorce standard of living" (p. 149).

Another important source of resiliency following the stress of divorce is the emotional bond with parents that "may buffer children from many of the strains associated with changes in family structure" (Amato, 1999, p. 149). Children who have had a functional relationship with a parent prior to divorce may be more resilient in that the relationship can provide some stability in the midst of change. Maintaining a close, functional parental bond is a way to manage the tension between intense dialectical forces. Adult children, then, are more able to cope with the acceleration of change following divorce when they have certain resources at their disposal.

The dialectical contradictions inherent in divorce create challenges for spouses as well as their children. The stability/change tension will be heightened as members abruptly exit and/or enter into the family boundaries. To deal with the drastic disruption to whatever form of stability it knew, the family will develop praxical improvisations. Remember our original discussion of selection, separation, neutralization, and reformulation in Chapter 1; families can generate examples of management strategies to cope with divorce. To manage the autonomy/connection dialectic using selection, for example, a couple may engage in legal battles to formally end their financial obligations, attempting to favor complete autonomy (i.e., disengagement) over connection. Partners who fail to pay child support after being court-ordered to do so are, in a way, enacting selection.

The family may enact separation strategies to manage the intense changes wrought by divorce. For example, family members may provide for some stability by keeping the house and neighborhood constant for the children while simultaneously recognizing changes in custodial care, as when one of the parents leaves the home. Families may neutralize the autonomy/connection dialectic by engaging inpublic events as a family but maintaining separate lives in private (e.g., parents living in separate quarters).

> *Family members may provide for some stability by keeping the house and neighborhood constant for the children while simultaneously recognizing changes in custodial care, as when one of the parents leaves the home.*

A family may choose to reformulate or reframe divorce. Some families may perceive divorce as a new beginning for the family rather than as an end. In so doing, they can manage the influx of change that occurs through divorce. This way of managing the contradiction of stability/change will determine, in part, the level of crisis that the family experiences through the divorce.

Whatever their response to divorce, parents and children will have to face the darkness of separation and loss. Although events that are not as terminal as divorce also pose challenges to the family, as with physical abuse, divorce is an obvious outgrowth of family disharmony. If family members do not deal with the challenges of family life, a holistic vision is not possible. Without the whole, a philosophy of family life based on partial visions, like those that prescribe what real families should do, will be distorted at best and destructive at worst. Although this means that families criticize, control, abandon, abuse, and destroy each other, it would be a mistake to focus only on the dark side. What makes family tragedy meaningful is the opportunity it provides to also bring out the best in people. Dialectically, family life is meaningful because it is a source of both darkness and light. In the next chapter, we'll take a look at the light of family life.

7

Bringing Light into Darkness

Family Spirituality

T his book has focused on using a dialectical approach to identify the structural and cultural diversity of the contemporary American family. Critical to taking this dialectical stance is to recognize the complex and contradictory nature of relationships within the family. In the previous chapter, we examined the evidence of the darker side of family life, and perhaps our examination created the false impression that *dark* can exist apart from its polar relationship with *light*. In this chapter, we focus on spirituality as a source of light in the family and use the terms *dark* and *light* to express the dialectical interplay of both forces. There is no dark without light. There is no light without dark. They exist simultaneously and, as with other dialectical tensions, we manage these through praxical improvisation.

Through an examination of the communication literature on spirituality, it becomes evident that rhetorical scholars have been more interested in exploring the subject than others. One of them, Miller, defines spirituality as "a personal experience that transcends human experiences and connects the human to a greater power or being" (2000, p. 174). We find evidence of spirituality in "praying, meditating, honoring the forces of nature, listening to instinctive responses, and seeking harmony within the self, the family, and the larger society" (p. 174). Furthermore, spirituality can govern "individuals in making decisions consistent with their values and help to overcome difficulties," making it "important to a holistic approach to family functioning" (p. 174). Spirituality, which is not to be confused with religion, indicates awareness of a benevolent and powerful presence beyond, but also interwoven with, the material world.

Although some people find it through religion, there are many ways to awaken spirituality within the family. Compared to religion, which is defined operationally in family studies as religious activity reflecting "an organized and creeded orientation toward a belief system," spirituality is more individualistic, less creedal, and

> *Spirituality, which is not to be confused with religion, indicates awareness of a benevolent and powerful presence beyond, but also interwoven with, the material world.*

"encompasses belief in a higher power, but one that may not meet the traditional view of a specific God-like being" (Miller, 2000, p. 174). Both religion and spirituality influence individual and family development. To the extent that individual family members develop and practice out of their awareness of a spiritual presence, the complexity of family relationships is multiplied. In other words, a relationship with a higher power creates an additional, transformational resource with which to manage the dialectical contradictions of life in the family.

❖ A SPIRITUAL APPROACH TO FAMILY

To organize ideas from various literature on spirituality and family communication, I outline here six emergent premises adapted from an earlier work (Sabourin, 1996). Although these premises are not exhaustive, nor are they mutually exclusive, they provide a starting place for a discussion of family spirituality and its role in the dialectical process.

Premise 1: Being a Family Is a Matter of the Heart

Professional experts on the family (e.g., researchers, teachers, and therapists) often assume that the family's success is determined by its skills in communication. But where does the power to communicate in a loving and nurturing way, even in the face of anger, fear, and doubt, originate? How do family members expand "the established contours of our hearts to include others in a permanent and life-altering way"? (Wright, 1989, p. 30). According to a spiritual approach, the power to love comes through a relationship with a higher being or force, however that may be defined—the goodness of the universe, divine love, Mother Nature, God, Buddha, or something else. As one communicates with a higher being or force through forms such as meditation, reflection, or prayer, "the enlightenment and the courage to communicate well" (Powell & Brady, 1985, p. 207) can emerge.

The intimate nature of family life means that members will be required at times to become vulnerable and transparent. Being in a family also means "we must be prepared to let a relationship change us" (Wright, 1989, p. 89). This is in direct contrast to the desire to control others and requires trust, not only in the human relationship but in a spiritual one. This is especially true when family members have previous experience with alcoholism, abuse, and/or divorce. Emphasizing a "letting go" approach in which family members let the relationship happen, rather than forcing a relationship by trying to make it happen, means taking a whole new stance in our thought and behavior patterns and in the dialectical management of family contradictions.

This premise of family spirituality shares common ground with the assumptions of *invitational rhetoric* (Foss & Griffin, 1995). Invitational rhetoric is an alternative approach to the study of interactional influence. Instead of emphasizing the intentional, dominating type of influence that is advocated by mainstream theories of persuasion, invitational rhetoric seeks to show how rhetors naturally and unintentionally influence each other through respect and acceptance. Both invitational rhetoric and spirituality adhere to the belief that communication is not about changing or controlling others but about allowing for "a relationship rooted in equality, immanent value, and self-determination" (p. 3). The purpose of communication, therefore, is not to dominate each other but to foster growth and to cultivate each other's spirits (Tukey, 1990). Spiritual approaches to family communication and invitational rhetoric show how interaction can be used "to manifest the Divine Ground, to allow the sacred and the profane to interpenetrate" (p. 68).

As a matter of the heart, family spirituality allows its members to adapt to change. Like the dialectical view, it recognizes that interaction transforms family members and their relationships in non-incremental ways. A more skills-based, logical approach to functional family development would emphasize controlling change, pacing slowly while maintaining balance and stability. By claiming its non-incremental nature, the spiritual approach adopts a dialectical stance toward the unpredictable, unbalanced, and transformational qualities of change, in addition to recognizing the desire for balance and control. When we consider the relationship with a spiritual force as a source of change that enables families to be channels of love and nurturing, the next premise emerges.

Premise 2: Human Communication Is Animated by the Divine

Most approaches to human communication place ultimate importance on cognition and behavior. Beyond human communication, however, we need mutual discernment of a higher power's presence to sustain family life toward its full potential. Awareness of the higher power can be mutually discerned through interaction within the family if members "lovingly listen to the self, to the other, and to God" (Wright, 1989, p. 99). As a result, we can see this higher being as a member of the family and a source of its empowerment. The spirituality of the family requires an unseen power to change lives, provide hope, and be a source of guidance. "The hidden power—the spiritual dimension of ourselves—is one of the important secrets to the success and strength of strong families" (Stinnett & DeFrain, 1985, p. 101).

As it is animated by the divine, or nonhuman, power, the human spirit is "a wide spacious area beyond the individual power to invent or control" (Moore, 1994, p. 67). Through intuitive processes, we can allow a connection to the oneness of spirit with others in this space beyond the tangible world. The actions of a family may not make sense to an outsider who is judging them by standards of logic, but they will make perfect sense to those with an awareness of their spiritual purpose. But because the inclusion of the spiritual dimension, along with cognitive and behavioral emphases, creates a paradigmatic shift in existing models of communication, it poses a threat to the traditions of science.

Spirit transcends both modern and postmodern conceptions of power and other (Smith, 1993). Power, which modernism portrays as a masculine, control-based force, is challenged by Other, the feminine voice of the postmodern. But Spirit, as a way to the future through the present, empowers through unity, replacing models of dominance and control and allowing for the highest good for all concerned to be the communicators' goal.

Without this awareness of the spirit through divine animation, Goodall (1993) laments that humans will remain "the only advanced species to regularly commit and glorify genocide, homicide, and suicide, when not busy watching television" (p. 43). Although they can choose dialectically to avoid or deny the presence of spirit through selection, they cannot permanently evade it. As with all dialectical forces, avoidance can only forestall change; it cannot prevent it. If we regard the family as a place where the material manifestation of consciousness with a divine interbeing is nurtured and expressed, it acquires a mysterious and nonscientific quality. The next premise elaborates on the notion of mystery.

Premise 3: Mystery: There Is More to Family Life Than Can Be Predicted, Explained, or Controlled

Much of what is known of the family comes from empirical research. Seeking to improve and control the family, this approach assumes that we can solve the mysteries of family relationships. To this extent, though, the nuances and subtleties of family life may go unnoticed and unexplored. This mystery, which arises in part from "the human impulse toward the apprehension of spirit" (Rushing, 1993, p. 162), is not recognized by social scientific theories of family. As Moore (1994) explains, social science tends "to see everything as if it were a machine, including our most precious relationships. As a result of this mechanization in our thinking, we've lost an appreciation for the mysterious factors that bring people together and force them apart" (p. xiii).

A dialectical approach, on the other hand, encompasses both the mysterious and the seemingly logical aspects of family life, allowing acceptance of its emergent spiritual qualities. For instance, to manage the contradiction of stability/change, a family may rely on faith. In so doing, they can simultaneously live with that which is unseen as well as that which can be seen.

The unseen, which requires faith to accept, is part of what drives change in the family. To the extent that they can achieve stability or predictability, family members can try to protect themselves from the uncontrollable consequences of change. In a way, practicing faith is a type of reformulation in that it can reframe the contradiction of stability/change as an opportunity to realize a divine, higher plan.

In this way, faith can be a light through the family's dark, mysterious times. In the principles of Al-Anon, a spiritually based recovery program for families of alcoholics, the following is said about the use of faith as a guide through change:

> Faith in a Power greater than we are helps us to use the Al-Anon idea with more confidence and result. For those of us who have lost our faith, or who have always had to struggle along without it, it is often helpful just to accept, blindly and with no reservations. We need not believe, at first; we need not be convinced. If we can only accept, we find ourselves becoming gradually aware of a force for good that is always there to help us. (Anonymous, 1968, p. 67)

Without an acknowledgment of the "eternal spiritual mystery as a source of quest and as a resource for personal growth, human beings are reduced to the role of psychological and social problem-solvers" (Goodall, 1993, p. 42). In terms of interactional dialectics, the family without this resource would select instrumentality over affection, denying the mystery of emotion that affection entails. They may, on the other hand, separate affection from instrumentality to manage its contradictory demands. Perhaps they would see faith as necessary to deal with times of crisis but logic as the way to deal with the routine. However its members decide to manage the mysterious nature of their relationships with each other and those in the larger environment, a family cannot forever deny that there is much that cannot be predicted or controlled. To broaden our thinking about how to embrace the unknowable, we continue with the next premise, which suggests that family communication is as much art as science.

Premise 4: Beyond Social Science: Family Communication as an Art

At times, there exists a blind acceptance of the positivistic values of social science, such as objectivity, observability, rationality, and atomism, as relevant to the study of the family. "Our books, magazines, and films are permeated with images of the family as a sociological construct or as a hygienic hothouse for human development" (Moore, 1994, p. 79). To move out from this limiting stance "requires a spiritual vision and a solid appreciation for the sacred" (p. 79). However, "Contemporary theories are secular and ignore the role of spirituality in human communication" (Tukey, 1990, p. 66). They "inflate the importance of cognitive, linguistic, and social processes beyond what is healthy for the individual" (Tukey, 1991, p. 5).

In the family, where spirits and souls as well as bodies and minds are housed, it takes more than technique to develop to its full potential. As Moore (1994) explains, the "key to giving the soul the family it wants . . . is to appreciate the poetry of what a family is" (p. 71). Through imagination, we can nurture the creative and poetic side of family life. In fact, Moore advocates immersion into the arts as a way to prepare for intimate relationships, and the sharing of the poetic as a way to honor rather than change them. Unlike social scientific goals for family life, "The soul is not dedicated to perfection. Work with the soul is not aimed at achieving an unblemished, unruffled relationship; on the contrary, it has an appreciation for human limitation and folly" (Moore, 1994, p. 71).

When social scientists prescribe how families should be, they rely on assumptions of homogeneity. The family that they have tended to conceptualize and study is based on mainstream demographics and values. Yet, if family is considered as art and science, allowing the creative to inform the logical, we find the ground beyond the purely cognitive, behavioral, and social biases of these assumptions. In family, where the potential for intimacy is greater than in any other group, this means that "love is a delicate art that requires many sensitive decisions" (Powell & Brady, 1985, p. 204). Accordingly,

> No one can tell you exactly how to keep healthy relationships alive, nor is this something that can be legislated or codified once and for all. Families need to be empowered to trust the wisdom of their own experience and to define what is life-giving and faith-enhancing for them. (Wright, 1989, p. 94)

Premise 5: Being a Family Goes Beyond the Material World

We sometimes define the spiritual as "the part of human nature where feelings, ideas, and morals are entered" (Stinnett & DeFrain, 1985, p. 161). Although many treatises on the family have failed to include its spiritual dimension, it exists nonetheless. From a rhetorical view, however, Tukey (1991) recognizes that the human self consists of four systems: the biological, the cognitive/affective, the social, and the spiritual. The symbols we use to create relationships "are more than social because humans are more than social creatures" (p. 3).

Even more directly, Goodall (1993) considers what a theory of communication would include "if we took seriously the idea that humans are, first and foremost, spiritual beings" (p. 40). The postmodern conception separates spirit from human and may lead the cynical to think that "what we really must be here for is for the accumulation of material things" (p. 43). Without a spiritual core, ethical and moral responsibilities can be ignored or denied. In other words, they are selected out from their inherent connection to the material. At an extreme, relationships with family can become only a place where "we do what we want, protect our materialism, and ignore the rest" (p. 43).

If those who are interested in studying the family fall prey to a limited conception of humans as nonspiritual, purely material beings and glorify rationality, ignoring the artistic, they will experience a failure to receive a full and rich vision of how families manage in their day-to-day lives. A discussion of the differences between the purely material concept, which Smith (1993, p. 266) calls "power," and one that incorporates an "other-worldly goodness," which he calls "spirit," illuminates further the dialectical necessity of incorporating both.

Power seeks to control others, whereas spirit, like invitational rhetoric, demonstrates truth. Furthermore, because power is material, science validates it but ignores spirit, which is incorporeal. We can observe power, but spirit is invisible. We can measure power, which is why scientists favor it, but spirit is ineffable, evading symbolic manipulations. Power is objective, whereas we discern spirit intuitively. Finally, whereas power exhorts, which results in prescriptions for families, spirit guides through example. Spirit attracts while power promotes. To sum, "The essential difference between power and spirit is that power . . . requires other people or material over which influence can be exercised. Spirituality has no such requirement and is most often thought of as an inner sense, such as grace" (Smith, 1993, p. 268).

Along with power, which often comes out through the dark side of family life, it is essential to include the spiritual when we attempt to provide a full description of the family's resources for managing dialectical tensions. As most social scientific approaches to the family do not incorporate the spiritual, they are, in a sense, incomplete. Although the dialectical approach does not make a point of including the spiritual as an essential resource and critical influence on family life, its conceptual frame allows for it to be integrated. The final premise reflects how this integration can take place.

Premise 6: Spirituality Is a
Unifying Force in the Midst of Diversity

In a study of 3,000 families seeking to identify their sources of strength, Stinnett and DeFrain (1985) found that those who were resilient to adversity were those who experienced "spiritual wellness . . . as a unifying force, a caring center within each person that promotes sharing, love, and compassion for others" (p. 161). As a unifying force, the spiritual dimension of family life helps members to embrace their wholeness, their good and their bad, revealing the principle of nonsummativity, that is, that the whole is greater than the sum of its parts. The whole is greater and can be accounted for through an inclusion of the spirit's animation of the family.

When we integrate the spiritual with the material, we can discover unity across all family structures and cultures, as well as unity with all living things including plants, animals, and the environment. In this way, "Rhetoric and symbol use guide us from our separateness toward unity and cooperation" (Tukey, 1991, p. 2). To attain unity, or connection, with all living things paradoxically requires autonomy to attend to the inner life for spiritual discernment. Through management of the inner, spiritual, world and the external, material, world, one can find "a sense of unity in multiplicity" (Goodall, 1993, p. 41). In this way, like a dialectical approach, a spiritual view of family transcends modern (i.e., power) and postmodern (i.e., other) divisions of communication (Rushing, 1993). Instead of dichotomizing, inclusion of the spirit "allows the realization of the inter-relationships among all things" (p. 159).

To manage the simultaneous demands of autonomy/ connection, families make praxical choices. One way to cope with competing demands is through selection, by which the family members avoid or ignore one of the dialectical forces in favor of the other. To exclude the spirit is also a form of selection; we are saying that it cannot be done away with, but it can be ignored.

But as Rushing tells us, "Without the spirit to remind power and other that they are not the whole, and indeed that they derive from the same source, their only possible relationship is agonistic" (1993, p. 166). The spiritual provides a vision that encompasses the whole and, like a reformulation strategy, reframes the competition between opposing forces of autonomy/connection. As a unifying force, the spiritual is a source for transcending the constant tension of relational polarity.

By applying these premises to a discussion of how families manage their darkness through the light of their spiritual natures, we develop an understanding of how inadequate a purely skills-oriented approach to problem solving is for creating deep change in highly embedded family patterns that reinforce and maintain problems. It becomes apparent that previous efforts by family experts to conduct research, develop theories, and formulate skills-based programs are critically limited by a two-dimensional world of power and other. The both/and nature of a dialectical approach allows incorporation of the spiritual, and in so doing can transform an understanding of family life.

To demonstrate how transforming the spiritual can be in guiding families through their darkness, we conclude this chapter with a brief examination of the spiritually based 12-step recovery programs that teach alcoholics and their families a surrender-based, rather than a control-based, management style.

❖ 12-STEP RECOVERY PROGRAMS

In 1939, a book was published that outlined a radically different approach to alcoholism. This book was called *Alcoholics Anonymous: The Story of How Many Thousands of Men and Women Have Recovered from Alcoholism*. The *Big Book*, its familiar title, was in its 24th printing as of 1986. A companion book for families of alcoholics, called *One Day at a Time in Al-Anon*, first published in 1968 and in its 24th printing as of 1986, outlines a spiritual way of life to help families to live with and overcome the negative effects of living with an alcoholic. Together, meetings of Alcoholic Anonymous (AA) and Al-Anon all over the world provide an effective way to manage the paradoxes of alcoholism through adopting a spiritual way of life.

The "12 Steps" of these recovery programs are suggestions for living a spiritual way of life to avoid being destroyed by alcoholism. As the *Big Book* states, though, "To be doomed to an alcoholic death or to live on a spiritual basis are not always easy alternatives to face" (2002, p. 44). This is especially true for atheists and agnostics who do not believe in a religious sense of a higher being. Part of the beauty of the 12-step approach, however, is that it leaves individuals free to determine their own sense of a higher power, even if that higher power is the group of alcoholics that attends their AA meeting with them. By not forcing or even allowing any discussion of "outside" issues such as religion, AA allows for all of its members to discover their own sense of spiritual power. The fact that they have been using alcohol as a higher power in the past is evidence that they have the capacity for faith.

In short, the steps to recovery from alcoholism for alcoholics and their family members begin with an admission of powerlessness (surrender) and continue through discovery and acceptance of a higher power (as they choose to understand that higher power) and an inventory process of recognizing harms done to others; making amends for wrongs done; developing a conscious contact with the higher power of one's own understanding; and then finally sharing their experience, strength, and hope with others who suffer from the family disease of alcoholism. As the *Big Book* (2002, pp. 44–45) states,

If a mere code of morals or a better philosophy of life were sufficient to overcome alcoholism, many of us would have recovered long ago. But we found that such codes and philosophies did not save us, no matter how much we tried.

We could wish to be philosophically comforted, in fact, we could will these things with all our might, but the needed power wasn't there. Our human resources, as marshalled by the will, were not sufficient; they failed utterly. Lack of power, that was our dilemma. We had to find a *Power greater than ourselves.*

As can be seen, the approach of the 12 steps offers a way to manage the dilemmas posed by alcoholism. It explains, for example, how dependence on a higher power can provide true independence of the spirit. It suggests that its members give freely of what they have in order to keep their own recovery. Alcoholics and family members alike are taught that to win with alcoholism, they must first surrender. In other words, these programs embrace the paradoxical nature of living with alcoholism and go beyond it to show how drinking is but a symptom covering a lack of knowledge about how to manage life's challenges. Although it differs from mainstream societal norms by stressing willingness over willpower to overcome problems, it is an effective way to help families who live with the disease of alcoholism. Because of its usefulness, the 12-step approach has been applied in the management of numerous other diseases and addictions, including gambling, overeating, smoking, workaholism, and codependency. It works through spiritual principles to shine a light on even the most troubled path. From an Al-Anon book of daily readings, one spouse of an alcoholic contributes the following:

During the days of active alcoholism every problem loomed so large that I was overwhelmed by it. It was the most important thing in the world. It was the final calamity. Hysteria was in charge. I must have known there was a world outside all this—a sane, comfortable way of living. But this was beyond me while I was wrestling with my daily shocks and despairs. Now that I have found Al-Anon, I look at my problems with a better sense of proportion and balance. I see problems worse than mine which my friends in Al-Anon handle with poise and courage. Thus my difficulties are scaled down to normal size; I know I can do something about them (Anonymous, 1968, p. 71).

Family life is rich with contradictions. To be intimate, for example, family members must "protect each other's solitude" (Moore, 1994, p. 6). To become stable, they must adapt to change. Each dialectical instance provides an opportunity for both growth and resistance to growth. In order to manage these paradoxical challenges, families often rely on logic alone. Some social prescriptions for creating an ideal family serve instead to cause confusion. Rather than face the facts of uncertainty and a lack of control, many family members and experts alike think the solution is to try even harder. The spiritual approach suggests that forcing solutions through willpower may contribute to, rather than solve, a problem that first requires acceptance.

A spiritual approach to the family seen within a dialectical framework provides infinite alternatives for accepting life as it happens, allowing its members to consciously act, rather than automatically react, to each other and to those outside of its boundaries. It presents a way to manage the dialectical forces of relationships creatively, spontaneously, and purposefully. Furthermore, because of the growing diversity of family structures and cultures within the United States, an even greater need exists for a way to appreciate and cultivate all that families have to offer. Recognizing an additional source of guidance, although itself a challenge, certainly makes the search for spirituality in the family worthwhile.

> *Family life is rich with contradictions.*

References

Abbott, S. (1985). *Codependency: A second hand life.* Center City, MN: Hazelden.

Allen, K., & Farnsworth, E. (1993). Reflexivity in teaching about families. *Family Relations, 42,* 351-356.

Allen, K. R., Blieszner, R., & Roberto, K. A. (2000). Families in the middle and later years: A review and critique of research in the 1990's. *Journal of Marriage and the Family, 62,* 911-926.

Allen, K. R., & Wilcox, K. L. (2000). Gay/lesbian families over the life course. In S. J. Price, P. C. McKenry, & M. J. Murphy (Eds.), *Families across time: A life course perspective* (pp. 51-63). Los Angeles, CA: Roxbury.

Amato, P. R. (1999). Children of divorced parents as young adults. In E. M. Hetherington (Ed.), *Coping with divorce, single parenting, and remarriage* (pp. 147-164). Mahwah, NJ: Lawrence Erlbaum.

Anderson, T. L., & Sabourin, T. C. (1996). *A preliminary analysis of conflict narratives in lesbian relationships.* Paper presented at the annual meeting of the Speech Communication Association, San Diego, CA.

Anonymous. (1968). *One day at a time in Al-Anon.* New York: Al-Anon Family Group Headquarters, Inc.

Anonymous. (2002). *Alcoholics anonymous: The story of how many thousands of men and women have recovered from alcoholism* (Rev. ed.). New York: Alcoholics Anonymous World Services, Inc.

Associated Press. (2001, December 31). New Year's Day bringing new laws. *Cincinnati Post,* 2A.

Baxter, L. A., & Montgomery, B. M. (1996). *Relating: Dialogues and dialectics.* New York: Guilford.

Bedford, V. H., & Blieszner, R. M. (1997). Personal relationships in later life families. In S. W. Duck (Ed.), *Handbook of Personal Relationships* (2nd ed.). New York: John Wiley.

Ben-Ari, A. (1995). The discovery that an offspring is gay: Parents', gay men's, and lesbian's perspectives. *Journal of Homosexuality, 30,* 89-112.

Bernardes, J. (1993). Responsibilities in studying postmodern families. *Journal of Family Issues, 14,* 35-49.

Bochner, A. P., Cissna, K. N., & Garko, M. G. (1990). Optional metaphors for studying interaction. In B. M. Montgomery & S. Duck (Eds.), *Studying interpersonal interaction* (pp. 16-31). Newbury Park, CA: Sage.

Bradshaw, J. (1988). *The family: A revolutionary way of self-discovery.* Deerfield Beach, FL: Health Communications, Inc.

Burnette, G. E. (1994). *Restoring peace to violent families.* Tampa, FL: The Spring of Tampa Bay.

Cargan, L. (1991). *Marriages and families.* New York: HarperCollins.

Chandler, T. C. (1986). *A profile of interaction in acute battering incidents.* Unpublished doctoral dissertation, Purdue University.

Charny, I. W. (1986). An existential/dialectical model for analyzing marital functioning and interaction. *Family Process, 25,* 571-589.

Cissna, K. N., Cox, D. E., & Bochner, A. P. (1989). The dialectic of marital and parental relationships within the stepfamily. *Communication Monographs, 57,* 47-61.

Clark, D. B., Kirisci, L., & Moss, H. B. (1998). Early adolescent gateway drug use in sons of fathers with substance abuse disorders. *Addictive Behaviors, 23,* 561-566.

Coleman, M., Fine, M., & Ganong, L. (2000). Reinvestigating remarriage: Another decade of progress. *Journal of Marriage and the Family, 62,* 1228-1302.

Coontz, S. (2000). Historical perspectives on family studies. *Journal of Marriage and the Family, 62,* 283-297.

Cordova, J. V., Jacobson, N. S., Gottman, J. M., Rushe, R., & Cox, G. (1993). Negative reciprocity and communication in couples with a violent husband. *Journal of Abnormal Psychology, 102,* 559-564.

Crocker-Lakness, J. W. (1996). *Stages of stepfamily development as transition points in spiritual growth as illustrated by the traditional Zen oxherding pictures*. Paper presented at the annual meeting of the Speech Communication Association, San Diego, CA.

Crocker-Lakness, J. W., & Sabourin, T. C. (2000). *Stepfamily development and spiritual growth: Creating an alternative model*. Unpublished manuscript, Department of Communication, University of Cincinnati.

Cronen, V. E., Pearce, W. B., & Snavely, L. (1979). A theory of rule-structure and types of episodes, and a study of perceived enmeshment in undesired repetitive patterns (URPs). *Communication Yearbook, 3,* 225-240.

Crosbie-Burnett, M., & McClintic, K. (2000). Remarried families over the life course. In S. J. Price, P. C. McKenry, & M. J. Murphy (Eds.), *Families Across Time: A Life Course Perspective* (pp. 37-50). Los Angeles, CA: Roxbury.

Fitzpatrick, M. A., & Wamboldt, F. S. (1990). Where is all said and done? *Communication Research 17*(4): 421-430.

Foss, S. K., & Griffin, C. L. (1995). Beyond persuasion: A proposal for an invitational rhetoric. *Communication Monographs, 62,* 1-18.

Gage, R. B. (1988). *An analysis of relational control patterns in couples.* Unpublished doctoral dissertation, Seton Hall University.

Gamache, S. J. (1997). Confronting nuclear family bias in stepfamily research. In I. Leven & Sussman (Eds.), *Stepfamilies: History, research and policy* (pp. 41-69). Binghamton, NY: Haworth Press.

Ganong, L. H., & Coleman, M. (1997). How society views families. *Marriage and Family Review, 25,* 85-106.

Giles-Sims, J. (1997). Current knowledge about child abuse in step-families. *Marriage and Family Review, 25,* 215-230.

Golden, T. (2000, April 23). Just another Cuban family saga. The *New York Times Magazine*, 62-67, 88, 95-96.

Goodall, H. L. (1993). Mysteries of the future told: Communication as the material manifestation of spirituality. *World Communication, 22,* 40-49.

Gottman, J. M., & Krokoff, L. J. (1989). The relationship between marital interaction and marital satisfaction: A longitudinal view. *Journal of Consulting and Clinical Psychology, 57,* 47-52.

Gottman, J. M., & Notarius, C. I. (2000). Decade review: Observing marital interaction. *Journal of Marriage and the Family, 62,* 927-947.

Graham, L. O. (2000). *Our kind of people: Inside America's black upper class*. New York: Harper Perennial.

Graham, M., Moeai, J., & Shizuru, L. (1985). Intercultural marriages: An intrareligious perspective. *International Journal of Intercultural Relations, 9*, 427-434.

Harvey, J., Wells, B., & Alvarez, M. (1978). Attribution in the context of conflict and separation in close relationships. In J. Harvey, W. Ickes, & R. Kidd (Eds.), *New Directions in Attribution Research, Vol. 2* (pp. 230-264). Hillsdale, NJ: Lawrence Erlbaum.

Heim, D. (1996, January 31). Family values, Christian values: A round-table discussion. *The Christian Century*, 104-111.

Hetherington, E. M. (1999). Should we stay together for the sake of the children? In E. M. Hetherington (Ed.), *Coping with divorce, single parenting, and remarriage* (pp. 93-116). Mahwah, NJ: Lawrence Erlbaum.

Horowitz, J. A. (1995). A conceptualization of parenting: Examining the single parent family. *Marriage and Family Review, 20*, 43-70.

Hrdy, S. B. (1999). *Mother nature: A history of mothers, infants, and natural selection*. New York: Pantheon Books.

Hughes, R., & Schroeder, J (1997). Family life education programs for stepfamilies. *Marriage and Family Review, 25*, 281-300.

Jorgenson, J. (1989). Where is the "family" in family communication?: Exploring families' self-definitions. *Journal of Applied Communication Research, 17*, 27-41.

Knowles, E. E., & Schroeder, D. A. (1990). Personality characteristics of sons of alcohol abusers. *Journal of Studies on Alcohol, 51*, 142-147.

Kurdeck, L. A., & Fine, M. (1993). The relation between family structure and young adolescents' appraisals of family climate and parenting behavior. *Journal of Family Issues, 14*, 279-290.

Laird, J. (1996). Family-centered practice with lesbian and gay families. *Families in Society: The Journal of Contemporary Human Services*, 559-572.

Lindbergh, A. M. (1955). *Gift from the sea*. New York: Pantheon.

Linker, J. S., Stolberg, A. L., & Green, R. G. (1999). Family communication as a mediator of child adjustment to divorce. *Journal of Divorce and Remarriage, 30*, 83-97.

McAdoo, H. P. (1998). African-American families: Strengths and realities. In J. Futrell, H. I. McCubbin, E. A. Thompson, & A. I. Thompson (Eds.), *Resiliency in African-American Families*. Thousand Oaks, CA: Sage.

McLoyd, V. C., Cauce, A. M., Takeuchi, D., & Wilson, L. (2000). Marital processes and parental socialization in families of color: A decade of review of research. *Journal of Marriage and the Family, 62,* 1070-1093.

McManus, M. J. (1994, Winter). Veil of tears: The church is part of our divorce problem—And solution. *Policy Review,* 50-57.

Menees, M. (1997). The role of coping, social support, and family communication in explaining the self-esteem of adult children of alcoholics. *Communication Reports, 10,* 9-18.

Miles, D. M. (1984). A model for stepfamily development. *Family Relations, 33,* 365-372.

Miller, J. E. (2000). Religion and families over the life course. In S. J. Price, P. C. McKenry, & M. J. Murphy (Eds.), *Families Across Time: A Life Course Perspective* (pp. 173-186). Los Angeles, CA: Roxbury.

Montgomery, B. M. (1992a). *A dialectical approach to reconceptualizing familial and marital relationship maintenance.* Paper presented at the annual convention of the Speech Communication Association, Chicago, IL.

Montgomery, B. M. (1992b). Communication as the interface between couples and culture. *Communication Yearbook, 15,* 475-507.

Moore, T. M. (1994). *Soulmates: Honoring the mysteries of love and relationship.* New York: Harper Perennial.

Murphy, B. C. (1998). *Difference and diversity: Gay and lesbian couples.* Binghamton, NY: Haworth.

Nakhaima, J. M., & Dicks, B. H. (1995). Social work practices with religious families. *Families in Society: The Journal of Contemporary Human Services, 53,* 360-368.

Olson, D. H., Sprenkle, D., & Russell, C. (1979). Circumplex model of marital and family systems I: Cohesion and adaptability dimension, family types, and clinical applications. *Family Process, 18,* 3-28.

Papernow, P. L. (1984). The stepfamily cycle: An experimental model of stepfamily development. *Family Relations, 33,* 355-363.

Pardeck, J. T. (1991). A multiple regression analysis of family factors affecting the potential for alcoholism in college students. *Adolescence, 26,* 341-347.

Patterson, C. J. (1992). Children of lesbian and gay parents. *Child Development, 63,* 1025-1042.

Patterson, C. J. (2000). Family relationships of lesbians and gay men. *Journal of Marriage and the Family, 62,* 1052-1069.

Phillips, R. (1997). Stepfamilies from a historical perspective. *Marriage and Family Review, 25,* 5-18.

Powell, J., & Brady, L. (1985). *Will the real me please stand up.* Allen, TX: Tabor.

Pyke, K. (2000). "The Normal American Family" as an interpretive structure of family life among grown children of Korean and Vietnamese immigrants. *Journal of Marriage and the Family, 62,* 240-255.

Rawlins, W. K. (1992). *Friendship matters: Communication, dialectics, and the life course.* New York: Aldine de Gruyter.

Rushing, J. H. (1993). Power, other, and spirit in cultural texts. *Western Journal of Communication, 57,* 159-168.

Sabourin, T. C. (1995). The role of negative reciprocity in spouse abuse: A relational control analysis. *Journal of Applied Communication Research, 23,* 271-283.

Sabourin, T. C. (1996). *Premises for a spiritual approach to family communication.* Paper presented at the annual convention of the Speech Communication Association, San Diego, CA.

Sabourin, T. C. (2000). *Visual portrayals of the real vs. ideal dialectic in early marriage.* Unpublished study, Department of Communication, University of Cincinnati.

Sabourin, T. C., & Stamp, G. H. (1995). Communication and the experience of dialectical tensions in family life: An examination of abusive and non-abusive families. *Communication Monographs, 62,* 213-242.

Scanzoni, J., & Marsiglio, W. (1993). New action theory and contemporary families. *Journal of Family Issues, 14,* 105-132.

Silverstein, L. B., & Auerbach, C. F. (1999). Deconstructing the essential father. *The American Psychologist, 54,* 397-407.

Smith, C. R. (1993). Finding the spiritual dimension in rhetoric. *World Journal of Communication, 57,* 261-271.

Smith, J., & Jones, B. (1999). *On the road to same-sex marriage.* New York: World Press.

Stafford, L. L., & Dainton, M. (1994). The dark side of "normal" family interaction. In W. R. Cupach & B. H. Spitzberg (Eds.), *The dark side of interpersonal communication* (pp. 259-280). Hillsdale, NJ: Lawrence Erlbaum.

Stamp, G. H. (1994). An appropriation of the parental role through communication during the transition to parenthood. *Communication Monographs, 61,* 89-113.

Steinmetz, S. K. (1985). The use of force for resolving family conflict: The training ground for abuse. *Family Coordinator, 26,* 19-26.

Stinnett, N., & DeFrain, J. (1985). *Secrets of strong families.* Boston: Little, Brown.

Teachman, J. D., Tedrow, L. M., & Crowder, K. D. (2000). The changing demography of America's families. *Journal of Marriage and the Family, 62,* 1234-1246.

Thompson, M. C. (1998). Indigenous resources and strategies of resistance: Informal caregiving and racial socialization in black communities. In J. Futrell, H. I. McCubbin, E. A. Thompson, & A. I. Thompson (Eds.), *Resiliency in African-American families.* Thousand Oaks, CA: Sage.

Thompson, P. (1993). *Emotional abuse: What it is and how it hurts us.* Center City, MN: Hazelden.

Trost, J. (1993). Family from a dyadic perspective. *Journal of Family Issues, 14,* 92-104.

Tukey, D. D. (1990). Toward a research agenda for a spiritual rhetoric. *The Journal of Communication and Religion,* 66-73.

Tukey, D. D. (1991). *A spiritual view of symbolic processes.* Paper presented at the annual convention of the Speech Communication Association, Atlanta, GA.

United States Census Bureau (2000). *America's families and living arrangement: Population characteristics.* Washington, DC: Author.

Ventura, C., Milholland, T., & Trujillo, D. (1994). *Intervention for men who abuse women.* Unpublished program manual. Cincinnati, OH: YWCA.

Walker, L. (1979). *The battered woman.* New York: Harper & Row.

West, R., & Turner, L. H. (1995). Communication in lesbian and gay families: Developing a descriptive base. In T. Socha & G. Stamp (Eds.), *Parents, children, and communication* (pp. 147-170). Mahwah, NJ: Lawrence Erlbaum.

Westerhoff, J. H. (1983). The church and the family. *Religious Education, 78,* 249-274.

Wright, W. M. (1989). *Sacred dwelling: A spirituality of family life.* New York: Crossroads.

Wynne, L. C. (1984). The epigensis of relational systems: A model for understanding family development. *Family Process, 23,* 297-318.

Yerby, J., Buerkel-Rothfuss, N., & Bochner, A. P. (1995). *Understanding family communication.* Scottsdale, AZ: Gorsuch Scarisbrick.

Index

About the Author

Teresa Chandler Sabourin is Professor in the Department of Communication at the University of Cincinnati. She received her Ph.D. from Purdue University in 1986. Her study of family communication began with a course taught by Edna Rogers at Cleveland State University, where she received her B.A. and M.A. degrees. She continued her formal study at Purdue and completed her doctoral dissertation on family violence. Since coming to the University of Cincinnati in 1984, Teresa has taught family communication several times a year. In addition, she has continued to do research on family violence and has published her work in journals such as *Human Communication Research, Communication Monographs,* and *Applied Journal of Communication.* She has also written several book chapters for edited collections on the topic of family violence. Teresa lives with husband Gary and son Clay in Cincinnati, Ohio.